The Diary of Jesus Christ

The Diary of Jesus Christ

BILL CAIN, SJ

ORBIS BOOKS
Maryknoll, New York 10545

ORBIS BOOKS
Maryknoll, New York 10545

Fathers and Brothers
MARYKNOLL™

Founded in 1970, Orbis Books endeavors to publish works that enlighten the mind, nourish the spirit, and challenge the conscience. The publishing arm of the Maryknoll Fathers and Brothers, Orbis seeks to explore the global dimensions of the Christian faith and mission, to invite dialogue with diverse cultures and religious traditions, and to serve the cause of reconciliation and peace. The books published reflect the views of their authors and do not represent the official position of the Maryknoll Society. To learn more about Orbis Books, please visit our website at www.orbisbooks.com.

Library of Congress Cataloging-in-Publication Data
Names: Cain, Bill, 1947- author.
Title: The diary of Jesus Christ / Bill Cain.
Description: Maryknoll, NY : Orbis Books, [2021] | Summary: "The Diary of Jesus Christ is a bold attempt to understand the person whom in excess of two billion people claim as their savior. These entries are not a gospel; they are something far more personal-not a third-, but a first-person account of the life of Jesus Christ"— Provided by publisher.
Identifiers: LCCN 2020036323 (print) | LCCN 2020036324 (ebook) | ISBN 9781626984073 (trade paperback) | ISBN 9781608338719 (epub)
Subjects: LCSH: Jesus Christ—Biography.
Classification: LCC BT301.3 .C35 2021 (print) | LCC BT301.3 (ebook) | DDC 232—dc23
LC record available at https://lccn.loc.gov/2020036323
LC ebook record available at https://lccn.loc.gov/2020036324

For Pete & Mary
For Paul & Nancy
For Kevin & Jack
For Jairo & Wade

Contents

Contents

Foreword

Bill Cain sent me a letter, some twenty years ago, during his teaching stint at St. Ignatius in Hunts Point, New York. He wrote, "Faculty somewhat trapped by the need for good behavior...when all that reveals God...is behavior itself. And if the kids trust us deeply, they will behave very, very badly. And not just to test the love, but because the rage in Hunts Point is extraordinary and why should they hoard it? Explode...and we'll pick up the pieces. When all is done, it will just be us—in awe of the size of what we all carry."

Homilies are supposed to inch us all closer to awe, which near as I can tell, is the opposite of judgment. Good homilies achieve this by breaking our hearts, making us laugh, and leading us to move beyond the mind we have. These homilies, found in *The Diary of Jesus Christ*, are good. They work on us in ways to which we are little accustomed. They soften us into a corner, then suddenly, we have new eyewear and see things in a wider frame. We've been waiting for this.

For a handful of years now, it has been a grace upon grace, that, as I report for duty every morning at 4:00 AM to address my emails, I will find, on occasion, one of Bill's homilies awaiting me. I savor them. I read them last. I let them wash over me. Like sacraments, they remind me to remember to keep first things recognizably first and to keep supple the mercy with which I long to lead. When St. Ignatius invites us to "see Jesus standing in the lowly place," Bill Cain helps us to visualize it. I don't feel the least bit enfeebled by guilt at the invitation. I "see" Jesus standing there and, with all the mess that the Incarnation promises, I know this is where the joy is. I *want* to stand there.

Once we are attentive to this longing to join Jesus, in the lowly place, we thrill at the marrow of the message. In these homilies we can see Jesus as one who lived and breathed and exuded a boundary-subverting inclusion—and it gives us hope. We see the endearments and the gestures, boxcars of tenderness that transport love to those places where they had not previously arrived. Perhaps, this is the "kryptonite" to the tribalism, division, and demonizing that hold us all in their thrall. This Jesus actually bumps into the social architecture that oppresses and into the privilege that keeps oppression quiet. And it happens by keeping us cheek to jowl with touch and tenderness, passion and whispers; with humiliation as our compass, and laughter as our north star.

Richard Rohr says that for St. Paul, "You do not live in the world and go to church. You live in the church and go to the world." Something gets fashioned through these snapshots of "Joshua" that compel us to step off the curb and into our world, eager to be in the world where God is: compassionate, loving, and kind. The Gospel says that Jesus grew in wisdom and stature and was favorable to God and just about everybody else. We experience this in Joshua's "early years" in the *Diary*, and we recognize the favor being highlighted in ourselves, pulled out of us when we least thought this possible. Love arriving where it's never been before. And we feel ourselves favorable. How did that happen?

The Jesus we see here is the mystic, the one who can spot wholeness in all our ruin and brokenness. Consequently, the mystic Jesus is never tripped up by behavior, but recognizes it as language. He's curious about it, so maybe we can be too. His mysticism says, "Explode...I'll pick up the pieces." Go figure...we then feel safe and can rest in the stillness of it. It really is not about "living in a church" but residing, as Bill says, "within the withinness of God." This is Joshua's address, and our yearning is to live here as well.

For thirty-five years, I've walked with gang members in Los Angeles at Homeboy Industries and have been fortunate enough to have my heart altered beyond its original shape. Many years ago, Bill showed me the beauty of standing in awe at what folks have to carry, rather than in judgment at how they carry it. On good days, when I've allowed myself to be reached, this insight of his has kept my mercy supple and my heart open. These homilies, housed in a diary, will work on you the same way.

The Magi are told, in a dream, to go home by another route. These tender pieces in this *Diary* ask the same of us. We choose the way, anew, that finds God in all "behavior" just waiting for us to lean into it and be eternally curious as we lean. The new path, presented here, frees us from the trap of "good behavior" and offers the lens of the mystical Joshua. Not a dispassionate view, dislocated from a humanity with its sleeves rolled up. It is a road hospitable to all that happens to us. There is no returning now by that earlier route, once you glimpse the spaciousness of this highway, this expansive God, "within the withinness" and welcoming us home, divinely present in all things.

It's hard to find better company than Bill Cain. On top of that, these homilies do what they are intended to do: widen what was narrow, open the restrictive, and galvanize folks to move beyond the mind we have. There is no intention to win some argument or fight some existing model. With an openhearted tenderness, it wants to fashion a new model. Like all homilies, we hear them, preached, as we gather, mindful of the union that is our longing and nature. One Christian is no Christian. We find ourselves, then, inextricably connected together in the hearing. We rise, afterwards, taking our leave from this exquisite gathering. We see as we are seen, loved without measure and without regret. Just us... in awe... picking up the pieces.

—Greg Boyle, SJ

The Calling

JOSHUA – AGE 9

Come to me, all you that are weary and are carrying heavy burdens, and I will give you rest. Take my yoke upon you, and learn from me; for I am gentle and humble in heart, and you will find rest for your souls. For my yoke is easy, and my burden is light.
—Matthew 11:28–30

When I was little—and I mean about nine—I wanted to be a rabbi.

This didn't have much to do with God.

Carpentry looked like a lot of hard work.

The only problem was that our particular rabbi never really seemed happy.

The happiest man in the village seemed to me to be the baker.

He was always cheerful. Always joyous. People were always happy to see him, which was pretty much the opposite of the way they felt about our rabbi.

The baker would carry on his shoulders a big yoke from which hung two sacks filled with breads of all kinds and, even though every household baked its own bread, people world scrape together their coins to buy his. His bread was exotic. He was Egyptian, and the Egyptians had mastered the art of making bread long before anyone else. But that wasn't the only reason people bought his bread.

He would make the women laugh, even my mother, and she wasn't always easy to get a laugh out of. It would be his way to toss in an extra roll for good customers. My mother would say, "You're trying to get me fat!" And he would say, "There's more of you to love." Old joke and not something my father could get away with, but, coming from Osiris, she would laugh.

We kids would follow him through town and he would shout at us.

"You're like a pack of cats at a fish market!"

But when he took off the yoke at the end of the trip through the village, he would give us the broken pieces of pastry for free. For the pleasure of it.

Ever since, I have associated bread with more than nourishment. Good bread is sheer pleasure.

The only time our baker wasn't welcome was Passover, when bread was a serious subject.

And it wasn't just the bread.

It was that he was Egyptian.

At Passover we looked on him with suspicion.

I thought we were good enough friends to talk about it, so I decided to confront him. I found him, alone and sad, in his shop and I asked, "Osiris, why did you keep us in slavery?"

He said to me, "Do I look five hundred years old that I kept you in slavery?"

And I said, "You know what I mean. Why did your people keep my people in slavery?"

He said bitterly, "Go ask your God why he killed our children to set you free. Go ask if that was fair."

We sat in silence.

And I knew I had no future as a rabbi.

I said, "Osiris, I don't think I am a very good Jew. I don't think I believe in a God that could kill children."

And he said, "Joshua, I don't think I'm a very good Egyptian. I don't want to be part of any people that could keep slaves."

Then he said, "But let's not be sad. Passover has passed over. I have bread to sell. Put on the yoke and carry it and let's sell the bread together."

When I put on the yoke, I was shocked at how heavy it was. I asked him how he could be so happy carrying such a heavy yoke. He answered, "Well, it's heavy only at the start. Once you sell the bread, it gets lighter. And the more you give away, the lighter it gets."

He was right.

So we went through the village, laughing and chatting, the burden getting lighter as more bread was sold and given away until there was no burden at all but only laughter.

That's when I knew what I really wanted to be.

A baker.

Simeon

JOSHUA – AGE 12

When the days were completed for their purification according to the law of Moses, the parents of Jesus took him up to Jerusalem to present him to the Lord. Now there was a man in Jerusalem whose name was Simeon, and when the parents brought in the child Jesus to perform the custom of the law in regard to him, he took him into his arms and blessed God, saying: "Lord, now let your servant go in peace; your word has been fulfilled: my own eyes have seen the salvation which you prepared in the sight of every people, a light to reveal you to the nations and the glory of your people Israel. Behold, this child is destined for the fall and rise of many in Israel. . . ."

—Luke 2:22–35

I ran away from home when I was twelve.

Did you know that?

Well, we were already away from home visiting Jerusalem. I stayed there when my parents went on their way home.

Parental neglect is a terrible thing.

But this wasn't that.

I told my mother I would be with my father and my father that I would be with my mother.

Oldest trick in the book.

But there was something that had to be done—in the temple and without them. You see:

Shortly after I was born, I was taken to the temple and offered to God—that was the custom, you just did it—but, my parents being my parents, they took it seriously.

So when the holy man of the temple told them I was something quite special—perhaps the Messiah—they took it to heart. They treated me as if I were in fact something special. Not that they wouldn't have without the prophecy—but the holy man's words intensified their expectations.

Sometimes, as a child, I could feel them watching me for something extraordinary to emerge, and this made me very uncomfortable from time to time.

I would ask, "Why are you looking at me like that?"

Finally they told me.

When I seemed ordinary enough—no signs that I was miraculous—I was something of a disappointment.

I tried very hard to meet their expectation. I studied scripture until I knew it chapter and verse. I prayed and prayed. Still, nothing special emerged except a scripture-spouting ordinary child who had bouts of temper from trying to be something he was not.

When I was twelve, they went back to Jerusalem to see if the old man—Simeon—was still alive.

A messianic check-up of sorts.

As we were walking up the steps to the temple, they saw him, exactly where they had seen him twelve years earlier, and doing the same thing—blessing a child.

While they were waiting to speak to him, they heard him say to parents of a newborn—word for word—what they thought he had said only to their own child. "Ah, such a special child. Now I can die in peace. I have seen the salvation of Israel." And the parents—as my parents had—gave the old man a few coins and moved on.

Joseph was not surprised. In fact, I think he might have suspected this all along.

My mother, however, was hurt. I could see that. Simeon saw the accusation in her eyes.

"You might remember our son," she said. "You said those same words about him years ago."

My parents left, but I stayed looking at Simeon.

There was shame in his eyes.

But I felt freed. Entirely freed.

My mind explored possibilities I could not even think of when I had been trying to meet my parents' expectations.

I knew I had to talk with Simeon on my own.

I contrived to stay in Jerusalem overnight and I knew I would have a day—a day at most— by myself in the Holy City. To buy my evening meal, I recited Torah—memorized by the yard—on a street corner. People were more than willing to toss me coins.

The next day, I sought out Simeon in the temple.

I found him, not offering blessings but sitting a dark corner —alone.

When he saw me coming, he expected me to accuse him. He shielded himself with his hands as if I were going to strike him.

He said, "I meant no harm. None at all. I offer blessings. That's all. And if I say the children are to be the Messiah, is it my fault if they don't turn out to be? . . .

"And who knows? Perhaps it is time for me to stop. Perhaps it is even time for me to fulfill my own promise and die."

Before I could respond to what he was saying, he went on, "I admit it. I'm a fraud. It's how I make my living. The other rabbis despise me for it. Stop hounding me. Go away."

I said, "I thank you for your blessing when I was a child, but I have so many questions I would like to discuss with a holy man—"

He said, "There are plenty of holy men in the temple. I'm afraid I'm not one."

I said, "I think you might be the only one, but let's not start there. There's too much on my mind."

And all the questions that had been pounding through my head during the night—and I suppose for years when I was trying to be good and unquestioning—began to pour out of me.

I asked, "It is said our parents Adam and Eve..."

"Yes," he said.

"They ate of the tree of good and evil?"

He said, "Yes and so we die."

I said, "Yes, because they ate of the *evil*. But what comes of eating of the *good*—which they also did. And far more of the good than the evil. Does that mean that in some way we do *not* die?"

He said, "I never thought of that." And he called other rabbis and we discussed that.

Then I asked, "If the ten commandments say killing is wrong, then how is the killing of the firstborn of Egypt right? Have we misunderstood?"

And the rabbis called other rabbis and we discussed that.

And I asked, "If we could build the pyramids as slaves, how come we do so little as free men and women?"

And the rabbis called still other rabbis and we discussed that.

Finally I asked, "In the scripture God speaks of Israel as if it were one single person. If that's true, is it possible—is it *possible* when the scripture speaks of the Messiah as *one* person— that he might be *many* people? Is it possible? Is it possible?"

"Yes," they said. "It is possible."

"Well, then," I asked, "is it possible that *every* child born is—in fact—a light to the nations? Is it possible that *every* child is destined for the rise and fall of the kingdom?"

They were quiet while they thought.

Then Simeon said, "You mean—you mean I was *right?*"

I asked again, "Is—it—possible?"

And the rabbis agreed that, yes, it was possible. And that they had never thought of that. And they looked on Simeon as something of a prophet.

And as Simeon was rejoicing, my parents arrived and they were furious with me. They shouted at me—which they never did. The rabbis tried to get them to stop, but I said, "No, please, let them go on." And they did.

And when it was finally time for us to leave, Simeon rose, full of pride, and said, "Child, before you go—"

And the old man took me in his arms and in front of the rabbis and my parents he proclaimed loudly, presenting me to the world, "Lord, now let your servant go in peace; your word has been fulfilled: my own eyes have seen the salvation which you prepared in the sight of every people, a light to reveal you to the nations and the glory of your people Israel."

My father slipped him a few coins, my mother continued to shout at me, and we went home.

Magnificat

JOSHUA — AGE 13

And Mary said,
   "My soul magnifies the Lord,
      and my spirit rejoices in God my Savior,
   for he has looked with favor on the lowliness of his
         servant.
      Surely, from now on all generations will call me
         blessed;
   for the Mighty One has done great things for me,
      and holy is his name.
   His mercy is for those who fear him
      from generation to generation.
   He has shown strength with his arm;
      he has scattered the proud in the thoughts of
         their hearts.
   He has brought down the powerful from their thrones,
      and lifted up the lowly;
   he has filled the hungry with good things,
      and sent the rich away empty."
                                    —Luke 1:46–53

She sang to me, of course, when I was a child. Sang to put me to sleep with my head in her lap. Sang to wake me up.

Many different songs, but always returning to one that was like a beautiful fairy tale.

My soul proclaims the greatness of the Lord. He has cast down the mighty from their thrones. He has filled the hungry with good things and sent the rich away empty.

As a child, I loved the vision she sang.

As I got older and began to notice that the realities around me didn't line up with my mother's song, I started to challenge the fairy tale.

She would sing, "*He has cast down the mighty from their thrones and has lifted up the lowly,*" and I would sing back, "*Maybe once, a long time ago.*"

She would sing, "*He has filled the hungry with good things and the rich he has sent away empty.*"

And I would sing, "*Maybe once, a long time ago.*"

When I would do this, she would look at me and say, "You know I wanted a girl, don't you?"

She said, "You know, you mock God for not filling the hungry, but what have you done for them?"

This was a cutting challenge because I knew what she did for them daily. No one was hungry if she could help it.

It hurt, too, because I knew that she believed I was destined for something great. Mothers were all told that their children might become the Messiah for whom we were waiting. The Messiah would tear apart the world as we knew it and bring about justice and peace.

Some of us hoped it would be us, but I didn't know how the Messiah could come out of a family like mine. My father wasn't a king or a priest. My mother wasn't a queen or a rich matron. They were poor people, and I felt they were something of a liability in the Messiah business.

But I honored her challenge.

I went to the marketplace.

I could see the injustice. Everyone could see it, with the rich buying food from the merchants who were making a killing while the hungry were begging for scraps. This was a situation that Isaiah tells us the Messiah would rectify, so I set out to rectify it. I took food from the stalls and gave it to the hungry. It seemed simple enough.

I wasn't exactly beaten up, but I was shoved hard enough to land in the dirt, stall after stall. By the time I came home, tail between my legs, fruit-stained and most un-Messiah-like, I was dirty, tired and ashamed. When I came in, I slammed the door behind me.

Joseph, my father, said to me, "What's wrong?"

I said, "Ask her," and went to my room.

She just smiled and sang her song.

It took me a week to formulate my plan, but I went back to the market and I sang her song.

I have a pleasant voice. Not cantor-quality, but good enough to have people toss money in my hat and, with the money, I bought food for the poor and some for myself.

The poor were very grateful and, as I ate with them, feeling moderately messianic, more came. In fact, they thronged. They looked at me as I ate my food. What could I do? I gave them what I had and went home hungry and angry.

As I came through the door, my mother was putting dinner on the table.

She said, "Eat." I sat down. I looked at the food. I looked at her.

I said, "This is a trap, isn't it? If I eat while others are hungry, I'm just another rich man. And if I don't eat, I'm just another hungry person who's part of the problem."

I stood and left the table.

My father said to my mother, "Do you know what's going on?"

She nodded and she sang her song.

I went back to the market, day after day, and sang and fed the poor and sang and fed.

Because I never had enough food myself and because there is no justice in the marketplace, my song became angrier and angrier. The angrier I became, the more the poor sang with me. The song became an anthem and people do not toss money into the hat when poor people are singing angry anthems. And, worse, you start attracting notice from the Romans.

A young centurion—I didn't see him coming—lifted me off my feet and put me up against a wall. Hard. He was around thirty and all leather and brass. I was all of thirteen and all skin and bone, but defiant. I said, "Put me down. All I'm doing is singing."

He said, "You? We could care less about you. What we need to know is the name of whoever taught you that song. Give me his name!"

I said, "What song? It's just a song."

He said, "*Pulling down the mighty from their thrones* is not just a song. It's treason. It's sedition. It's an attack on the Empire. Who taught you that subversive song? Who wrote it? Because whoever wrote that song is trying to topple Rome."

I started laughing. I said, "Topple Rome? You're joking."

He banged me against the wall. I stopped laughing. He said, "You are being used, and whoever is using you is a very dangerous person."

When he saw I was seriously baffled, he relented. He explained to me what the song meant. That everything had to change. That the rich would lose their possessions. That their power would evaporate. That a new world would appear. In short, treason to him; the Messiah to us.

I was astounded. Speechless. I couldn't form words. After a while, he assumed I was a half-wit and let me go with a warning.

"Give me the name of whoever wrote that song, son, or you will have to answer for it. And never sing it again if you know what's good for you."

I went home in a sort of trance. I came in the door quietly. I looked at my mother and walked to my room without saying a word and went to bed. My father said, "I'm lost. You?" She nodded that it was all right.

Later, my mother came into my room with bread and soup. She put the food on the table at the side of the bed and said softly, "Eat. You need to eat. There's no shame in eating."

I looked at her and said, "Who *are* you?"

She said, "There are days I feel like asking you the same question."

I said, "No, really. Who are you?"

She said, "I'm your mother, though there are days I do not feel treated as such."

I said, "No. That's not what I mean. Are you the Messiah?"

She said, "I think everyone is born the Messiah until they disqualify themselves."

I thought about that. I thought about all that had happened.

I asked, "Have I disqualified myself?"

She said, "Absolutely not. What you did in the market-place was very brave."

I shook my head. "No. Have I . . . Have I disqualified myself from being your son?"

"That," she said, "would be impossible. No matter how big you get, or how surly, or how messianic, you will always be my son."

I asked, "Who taught you that song?"

She said, "It's not entirely original. It's made from bits and pieces of things that I like."

"Did you write it," I asked, "to bring down the Roman Empire?"

She said, "Perhaps incidentally. I wrote it to enlarge my soul. Each time I sing it, my soul becomes larger."

I nodded.

I said, "Would you sing it to me?"

I put my head in her lap as I had when I was a child.

She sang and, as always happened when she sang her song, my soul became larger.

The Women of Bethlehem

JOSHUA – AGE 15

When Jesus realized that they were about to come and take him by force to make him king, he withdrew again to the mountain by himself.

—John 6:15

I went to my father when I was young and informed him that I knew what I wanted to be when I grew up.

He said, "And what's that?"

I said, "I want to be a king. What do you think about that?"

He said, "Talk to your mother."

I said, "No. I want to know what you think."

He said, "Your mother will tell you what I think."

So I told my mother I wanted to be a king.

She said, "King? You can't even keep your room clean."

I said, "If I were a king I wouldn't have to keep my room clean. Someone would clean it for me."

She said, "Then it wouldn't be your room. You can only be a king over what you actually can rule."

I told my father what she had said.

He said, "See. That's exactly what I think."

They had their act perfected. I could get by either one of them, but together, I didn't have a chance.

So I asked my father, "What do you really think?"

He said, "I think there has never been a good king. Ever. They are all corrupt. I hate kings."

It was uncharacteristic of my father to hate anything, but this hate was pure.

He asked, "Why do you want to be a king?"

I said, "So I can do anything I want."

He said, "You can do that now. Try. Do what you want. But don't think just of making your life easier. Actually think about what you really want to do."

So I tried.

I wanted to make really beautiful furniture. A chair and a table. I worked through the night. Many nights. When I discovered how demanding it is to do what you want, I gave it up. It was just too hard.

Shortly after that, I forgot about becoming a king.

When I was fifteen, I wanted to see more of the world, and this was something that was considered odd. People did not leave their villages unless it was necessary, but I wanted to take a trip. So I took a week and walked where my feet took me.

When I found myself in Bethlehem, I thought I would try to find where I was born. I knew the story. The inns that had been full. The stable. The star.

The first thing I noticed was that girls—young women, my age—were giving me the once over. Heads were turning.

I thought I might like Bethlehem.

I went into a tavern. The young woman behind the bar was just about my age. She asked me what I wanted and then, smiling at me, she served me and asked if she could join me. This never happened in Nazareth.

I thought I might stay in Bethlehem for a while.

She asked where I was from.

I said, "Nazareth," and she seemed fascinated. There is nothing fascinating about Nazareth. "Can anything good come out of it?" is the saying. So it had to be me she was interested in.

Another young woman joined her. We drank and talked.

She thought I was fascinating too.

Finally, I said, "Yes, I'm from Nazareth, but actually, I was born here."

This puzzled them.

They asked when.

I said, "I can tell you exactly. It was at the time of the census."

When they fell silent, I asked, "What's wrong?"

The first girl looked to the second and said, "I'll go and get my mother."

When I asked again what was wrong, the remaining girl smiled and said, "The mothers will explain better than we can."

We sat in silence until the girl returned with her mother. She sat down at the table and looked at me very seriously. A small group of other women came with her and stood at the door and stared.

The girl's mother asked me to repeat what I had said to her daughter.

I said, "I was born here at the time of the census."

The woman said very seriously, "Child, that's impossible."

I said, "I don't think my parents would lie to me."

She said, "All the children—all the boy children—born in Bethlehem were killed at exactly that time."

I said, "All? All of them?"

The women didn't even have to nod their heads for me to know this was true. I asked them to tell me the story.

"The king," she said. "King Herod heard there was a prophecy that one of the children born in Bethlehem would become a king himself, a king who would dethrone him. So he had all the boys under two killed.

"The soldiers were very thorough," she said. "Very thorough. There was no way a child could have escaped. No matter where we tried to hide our children, they were found. There was a terrible sadness. For some years after, no children at all were born here.

"We went mad. All of us. The grief was so intense that one of the soldiers who killed our children came back and killed himself here in the street. No one was immune. So you must be wrong, young man. No one escaped. There are no young men your age in Bethlehem."

More mothers arrived and circled me.

They began to lay their hands on me very gently.

"My boy would be your age now," one said. And another, "Yes, but he wouldn't be as tall." Or "He would be taller." Or "fairer." Or "darker."

I felt like weeping.

One mother said, "Everyone knows I was a cranky woman even before the deaths. My little boy would look at my cranky face and imitate it and make me laugh. So don't cry, little one. Make me laugh, son. May I call you my son?"

I said, "My privilege, mother."

They wanted to touch me and look at me and hold me.

And, of course, they fed me.

One woman, who arrived shortly after, remembered a family that had passed through at the time of the census. She took me to the stable where I was born. A hut really. If you had been a donkey or a sheep or a dog, it would have been perfectly adequate. They could tell I was ashamed.

They all said, "Never be ashamed. Perhaps it was because this hut wasn't fit for a child that it saved you. You are our hope. You are what our children could have been."

I embraced them and they held me tight.

As I embraced the girls my age, they whispered, "Goodbye, my brother…" "My little brother…" "My big brother…"

I went home to my parents and asked my mother about it. She said, "Talk with your father."

I asked him why they had never told me about this.

He said, "But we did."

I said, "No. I would remember."

He said, "Do you remember when you broke your arm?"

I said, "Of course. I fell off the roof. "

"What were you doing on the roof?" he asked.

"I don't remember. But one day…no, it was night…"

"What were you doing on the roof at night?"

I had no answer.

He said, "You didn't fall. You jumped. That was your reaction to the story. You heard your mother and me talking one night and forced us to tell you the story. We hoped you'd forget. We never brought it up again for fear that it would drive you mad as it almost did us. By the way, please never bring this up to your mother again. Such terrible suffering. And for what? The fear that one child might escape and become king."

I asked, "Am I to be a king?"

"Fortunetellers, seers, prognosticators—stay away from them," he said. "Even if you don't believe them, they can plant seeds that corrupt and change you. If you need to listen to someone, listen to the women you met. What did you feel in your heart when they were talking?"

I said, "I felt I was their son.

"I felt their love for me was generous; there was no envy or bitterness in it.

"I wanted to fix their houses.

"I wanted to serve them.

"And make them laugh again after long sorrow.

"I wanted to hear their stories and tell their stories and heal the wounds in their hearts.

"I wanted to sit at their tables and eat till I burst.

"I wanted to be their son for them.

"I wanted to be worthy of their love.

"I wanted them to be one family.

"I wanted to bring them here for them to meet you.

"I wanted to bring down the kings that would hurt them.

"I wanted them never to be hurt again."

And my father asked, "This is what you really want?"

I said, "Yes. This is what I really want to do."

"Fine," my father said.

"Do exactly what you want to do."

Woman of the Parables 1

JOSHUA — AGE 17

He told them another parable: "The kingdom of heaven is like yeast that a woman took and mixed in with three measures of flour until all of it was leavened."
—Matthew 13:33

We were carpenters, my father and I, but we also worked in the building trade.

We mostly did the wooden roofs, but I also worked on stone walls. Shoving stones into place is hard work. I became strong through lifting, hauling. Those houses I made made me. The swing of a hammer. The driving of a nail. I used to be more muscular than I am now. Preaching and walking? It's soft work by comparison. I miss serious work.

When I was apprenticing, after the work of the day was done, my mother used to volunteer me to do repairs on people's houses. The contractor we worked for was unscrupulous, so my mother never objected when I stole materials from his building sites. Reparative justice, I suppose.

There was one old woman to whom my mother often sent me. "Crazy Ruthie" had earned her name over the years. It was just what we called her. There was no meanness in it.

And Ruthie gave as good as she got. She could drive me mad.

I would return home from working on her house and complain to my mother. I'd repair a wall, and then another wall, and then another, and then she'd have me go back to the first wall and rebuild that. After a while, I had replaced so many stones in her house that there wasn't an original stone left in it. After I had entirely rebuilt the building, which looked exactly the same as when I started, I asked my mother why she kept sending me there.

My mother said, "You'll figure it out or you won't."

At this time, during my teenage years, I was a very observant child. I thought that, by pleasing my rabbi, I was achieving holiness. Since I could recite Torah by the yard, I was the teacher's pet and was very honored when he said he would come to have dinner in our house.

The morning of the dinner, before I left for studies, I asked my mother to cook a good meal.

"Don't I always?" she replied.

Then I asked her to promise to behave.

She nodded noncommittally.

When I brought my rabbi home that night and opened the door, there was Ruthie.

I looked at my mother.

She looked at me.

She said, with a perfectly straight face, "She's a very good cook. And she's the best baker I have ever known."

Surprisingly, Ruthie prepared an astonishing meal.

The only problem was, she wouldn't eat from her own plate.

She was eating from the rabbi's plate.

My mother didn't seem to notice.

The rabbi did.

Then, when I thought things couldn't get worse, Ruthie said, "You know, rabbi, I've never liked the Torah," and I choked.

My mother said calmly, "And why is that, Ruthie?"

Ruthie said with a sigh, "I like a love story."

The rabbi said, "There are many love stories in the Torah."

Ruthie said, "Yes, but it's not really a *love* story."

He said, "The love of God."

Ruthie said, "Oh, him. What use is he?" and I died a little inside.

Ruthie asked my mother, "Do you have a love story?"

My mother pointed at me (I was bright red with rage and embarrassment) and said, "Him."

Ruthie asked the rabbi while picking a radish from his plate, "What about you, Rabbi?"

He said, "My wife and I, we have many children. Each one of them is a love story."

And the rabbi asked, "What about you, Ruthie?"

She said, "Oh, yes, I have a love story. My husband and I were a love story. Oh, he was a handsome man and I was a lovely girl. But I'll tell you a secret. I was a bit crazy when I was younger, you see. People used to call me Crazy Ruthie. Don't tell anybody. Well, he—my husband—got tired of taking care of me. He left."

The rabbi said, "That's very sad."

She said while nibbling an onion, "Not really. I had love. And his new wife is lovely. She and I talk sometimes, and sometimes they bring the children over and let me play with them."

The sheer generosity of that stunned us.

Ruthie went on matter-of-factly eating from our plates, though we had stopped caring.

"You see," Ruthie said, "my soul is too big for my body. I can't keep control of it. It's a problem."

We ate the rest of the meal in silence.

When the rabbi was leaving, he said, "Come on, Ruth. I'll walk you home."

She said, "Fine, but you can't come in. The house is falling down and nobody will help me fix it."

When they left, my mother and I sat in silence for quite some time.

Finally my mother said, "Do you understand?"

I said, "I understand you ruined the evening."

"Did I?"

I said reluctantly, "No."

Then I said, "I'm going to have to rebuild her house until one of us dies, aren't I?"

She asked, "Why?"

"Because," I said resentfully, "her house is as much the temple as the Temple is."

She waited.

I said with some admiration, "More. Because she makes it holy on her own, it's just her and God."

She waited.

I said, "And because she's irreplaceable. Unrepeatable. Unique. Of unlimited worth, it's not just her and God. It's just God."

My mother said, "I knew you would get it eventually," and she got up to wash the dishes.

So I rebuilt Ruthie's house again and again. I got to enjoy it. I got to know the special places in it. The nooks where she kept memorials of her husband and the children that were not her children. And I grew to love that house as I did many houses I worked on.

I built many houses.

Dwelling places.

Ruthie came to hear me preach one day. At the end she said, "You have to give this up. The rain is pouring in my roof. Come home and do something useful."

I said, "This is my work now, Ruthie."

Ruthie looked concerned.

She asked, "But where's your love story? Don't neglect your love story. You ought to hook up with that woman from Magdala. She's out of your league, but from the way she looks at you, I think she might have you."

I laughed.

Then she said, as sanely as anything I had ever heard, "Don't let it go too long."

She was one of the women who was there when I actually became the stone that the builders rejected.

She was there when the tools of my trade were turned against me and wood and hammers and nails became the enemies of my body. When these things that had helped shape me came at me to destroy me.

She stood with the sobbing women but Ruthie did not cry.

She looked at me like she understood.

When I passed over…when I found I could dwell anywhere…when walls and doors and locks and keys were no longer a concern, I found myself sitting on Ruthie's bed on her neatly folded woolen blanket.

I watched Ruthie go through her rituals. Touching mementos. Dolls. Broken cups. Faded embroidery.

I said, "Hello, Ruthie."

She said, "Have you come to fix the roof?"

I said, "Yes. That's exactly why I came."

"Well," she said, "there are other things that need to be done as well."

I said, "I'll get busy then."

She said, "Don't," and she laughed. "There was never any need. Poor boy, how many times did you build this little house?"

"Many," I said.

She said, "I just wanted your company. You were a handsome young man and you reminded me of my husband. Did I ever tell you about my husband?"

"Yes, Ruthie," I said. "You did."

I asked, "Did you see what happened to me?"

She said, "Oh yes."

I said, "You didn't seem upset."

"I saw it coming," she said. "It's what happens when your soul gets bigger than your body. People become frightened. You used to be frightened of me."

"No more," I said.

She said, "Well, your soul is bigger now, isn't it? It's why you can be here. Dwelling among us."

I said, "Us?"

"Oh, yes," she said. "Elijah comes to visit. And your cousin John drops by. And my husband. And all the children

I never had. Many of the prophets. My namesake, Ruth. Sometimes it gets quite crowded in here. Would you like me to introduce you to everyone?"

I said, "I would like that very much."

She said, "One question first. It's the only question worth asking really..."

I waited.

"Did your life ever become a love story?"

I said, "Yes, Ruthie, it did."

She asked, "Who did you love?"

I said, "I'm here, aren't I?"

And I went to work on the roof.

Heaven or Helen

JOSHUA — AGE 25

The Son of Man came eating and drinking, and they say,
"Look, a glutton and a drunkard, a friend of tax collectors
and sinners!" Yet wisdom is vindicated by her deeds.
—Matthew 11:19

The hardest thing I had to give up to find God was religion.

I was good at religion. I kept the commandments. Not just the 10. I kept all 613 commandments of the law. I kept them well. No one called me a drunkard then. I was holy.

I was an Essene. I had joined the monastic community in the mountains and it was wonderful. Peaceful. No women. All men. We wore perfect white robes; we kept the law; three times a day we washed completely. We were beautiful. And thin. Clean and pure, I lived austerely for three years. I could have done it for a lifetime. I probably would have—if it hadn't been for Helen.

It was Helen's fault I left.

Helen died.

I asked permission to go to her funeral and, permission denied, I decided to ask for forgiveness instead. It was the first time I had ever broken a rule, but Helen had been a second mother to me. How could I not be at her funeral? And I was sure I could get back before dawn.

Helen was a Greek. She converted to marry Solomon, but, in her heart, she remained a Greek. She lived like a Greek. She cooked like a Greek. I ate forbidden food at her house.

Moussaka.

Have you ever had moussaka?

You can't image the effect that just seeing moussaka has on someone who has been brought up strictly kosher.

Helen would say, "You should taste this before you die. No one is making you. No one is even asking you. But it's here and I'm going to clean the bedroom."

Helen never really adjusted to Jewish ways.

"Statues," she'd say. "I miss statues. Why don't you people have statues?"

"Well," I'd tell her, "God forbids us to make graven images."

"That doesn't seem fair when he makes images of himself all the time."

"Like what?" I asked.

"Well, there's you, little one. There's me. There's Sol..." She paused and, laughing, added, "though he didn't do a very good job on Sol."

Sol would agree. "No," Sol would say. "But he did very well when he made you." And she would say, "Yes. He did."

Sol would say, "I was a good Jew when I met you. Now look at me. I break all the rules." And she said, "When I die, you can repent and become holy like little Joshua here. But please, wait till I am gone."

Sol's real religion was Helen and her religion was *eros, agape, filia*—all those kinds of love the Greeks have words for and we don't.

As she got older and lost her beauty, she would say, "If people live together enough, they start to look like one another. I was hoping Sol would come to look like me. But what can you do? I look more and more like Sol every day!"

Some of their children took after her; some, after Sol. But they all were loved and knew it, so they grew up sure of themselves—which is its own kind of beauty—and that made for a family resemblance. I was adopted into their household. She was my second mother. So I snuck out in the dark of night.

When I got to her house, we all wept for Helen, and we all laughed. And the crowd all drank until they were laughing and crying at the same time, which Helen would have enjoyed.

After all the others left, it came down to just Sol, the children, and me.

Sol offered me moussaka.

I turned it down.

He offered me wine.

I turned it down.

He said, "Really, little one? You won't drink with me?"

I said nothing. Even had I not lost my appetite for rich food and drink, I couldn't have taken his offer. My self-respect wouldn't have allowed it. Such impurity would have made a mockery of my robes. I let my sunken cheeks and my deep monastic silence answer for me.

Sol spoke again, "You really should drink with me tonight because … because … because it's your last chance."

I said, "Sol, you have many good years in you yet."

He looked at his children and said, "We all know that isn't true. I'm the kind that dies six months after. And everybody will say, 'He was weak,' and I am. Helen was the strong one. So drink with me because you will never see me again."

I didn't drink.

He nodded and said, "Drink with me, little one, drink with me now because you will never see me again—not even in the afterlife."

I said, "Don't say that."

Sol said, "If I become a devout Jew, what will happen to me when I die?"

I said, "You will go to the bosom of Abraham."

And he asked, "And where will Helen be?"

I said nothing because we all knew the answer. Helen had never really given up her false gods. She kept her statues in the bedroom. In the afterlife, she would not suffer, but she would not be with Abraham and there would be a gulf between them. And he said, "If it comes to a choice between heaven and Helen, I want to go to Helen."

And I didn't drink.

Then the oldest of his sons stood and said, "Drink with me tonight, little holy one, because you will not be seeing me in the afterlife either."

And the other children raised their glasses and said the same.

And Sol said, "Drink tonight. Drink with all the people who you may never see again for all eternity. Drink with us tonight, because none of us will be there in your clean and perfect heaven."

I didn't make it back to the monastery that night.

Or early morning.

When I did get back, my robe was stained badly with wine. And vomit. And urine. And the mud of the road.

This was the first time—though not the last—that anyone ever called me a drunkard.

And, of course, he was right.

As I removed my robe and laid it at my teacher's feet, I said, "Don't disturb the peace of the monastery. Don't waste your breath. I just came to say goodbye."

He said with concern for me, "You will never find God out there."

"Well," I said, "then I suppose God will have to find me."

And—naked—I left the monastery.

And God's search for me began in earnest.

29

JOSHUA — AGE 29

Jesus was about thirty years old when he began his work.
—Luke 3:23

One night I heard my parents talking. The conversation went like this:

My father said, "He's twenty-nine years old. What's he doing still living at home?"

My father was never one to criticize, so this took me by surprise.

My mother said, "He's preparing."

"For what?" asked my father. "What do you prepare for that takes twenty-nine years?"

She said, "He's building up to something great."

My father replied, "You put too much pressure on him. You always have. You expect too much. It's the fault of that man in the temple."

My father continued, "It's my fault, actually. He should have grown up with your gifts. But he grew up ordinary. Like me."

After my father passed away, my mother and I didn't talk about him much. She would occasionally forget and set him a place at dinner and seem surprised when he didn't show up. Perhaps she did that on purpose.

My mother is not anyone's image of a spiritual woman. She is practical. She stays busy. She stays away from temple. She's much too busy with the house and the neighbors. She rarely prays in the traditional sense.

One night, I asked her, "What did the man in the temple say to you about me?"

She said, "It was a long time ago."

I waited.

She said, "Don't you remember?"

Still I waited.

She said simply, seriously, "He said, 'The salvation of the world depends upon you.'"

Shortly after that, I went into the desert.

My mother was polite about my going into the desert, but not enthusiastic.

In the desert, I tried to fill myself with God. I tried to become a burning bush; a pillar of fire; the plagues of Egypt; the warrior God. I tried to fill myself with curses as I had seen my cousin John do. He could place a curse and the curse would stick like a burr in people's consciences.

I failed.

I was miserable. I almost lost my mind. I was terrified and hungry and thirsty and, above all, I was brutally lonely. Lonely as I had never dreamed a person could be.

I don't know what I was expecting to be given there. A new set of engraved stone tables, like Moses? A scroll sweet as honey to eat, like Ezekiel? Daniel's writing on the wall?

29

When I came out of the desert forty days later—lonely, hungry and exhausted—my mother welcomed me home without an I-told-you-so. She took care of me without asking questions.

As she cooked me a meal, I said to her, "I'm sorry. I've failed."

She said, "Failed? In what have you failed?"

I said, "I have turned out to be ordinary. Ordinary like my father."

She said, "There was nothing ordinary about your father."

We sat in silence.

Then she asked, "Did anything extraordinary happen while you were there?"

I said, "Before I left the desert, I was visited by an angel."

Because she was such a practical woman, I expected her to mock me. She didn't. All she said was, "Oh?"

I said, "It may have been a delusion. Do you think it was a delusion?"

She asked, "Did he speak?"

I said, "Yes."

She asked, "What did he say?"

I said, "He said...he said to give you his regards. 'Give my love to your mother for me,' is what he said exactly."

She didn't say anything.

I asked, "Mom, has an angel ever visited you?"

She said, "Did he say anything else?"

I said, "You're not surprised?"

She said, "What else did he say?"

"He said that Joseph isn't my father."

She nodded. "And..."

"And," I said, "that God filled you and created me out of the stuff of godhead."

35

She said, "He said all this? He was in a very talkative mood."

I said, "I think he was glad of the company. I know I was. But none of it was in words."

She said, "What was it if not words?"

"It was like I was a musical instrument and he was playing me. That all that he told me was already in me and the information came out of me like a song as he played me, but it was all so charged with feeling that it could only be music."

She asked, "What instrument?"

I said, "When he was talking about you, a flute. About Joseph, a muted trumpet. About me, a drum so large it shook the world. In fact, the drum may have been the world.... How was it for you?"

She nodded and said, "The same—flute, trumpet, and drum. But the drum was very faint. A heartbeat in the womb. Did he say anything else?"

I nodded. "He said...he said that I am God's son."

She said, "What did you say?"

"About Joseph, I said, 'You're an angel. You know nothing about families. Joseph is as truly my father as you are an angel.' About me being made of the stuff of God, I said, 'What else would anything be made of?' About being God's child, I thanked him for the reassurance. I knew that everyone I had ever met, even the Romans, were God's children, but I had never been entirely sure about myself."

She said, "And the angel said?"

"He said, 'You know you're very like your mother. You have an answer for everything. When I appeared to her and told her she would be the mother of the savior, she said, 'Really? How?' It stunned me. People don't usually ask questions of an angel. She made me sit down at the kitchen table and explain it all to her. I never had to account for myself before."

"I said, 'I have spent many hours at that table.'

"Then he said, 'Give your mother my regards. Apologize to her for me. I was doubtful about entrusting the salvation of the world to a young girl, but she has taught you better than an angel could.'"

My mother said, "To be fair, what do angels know except happiness? And happiness is a poor teacher."

"I asked him what my message to the world should be. He said to ask you."

She said, "You mustn't be disappointed in angels. They're very limited in what they can do. And their days are numbered."

I asked, "Why?"

She said, "Well, they are messengers. We won't need messengers once we realize that we are the message."

"He said that you are a good teacher."

She shook her head and said, "Not when it comes to you. Try as I did, you were always running off to the temple to find God. I did my best. Still, you had good teachers in the desert. Hunger. Thirst. Loneliness. They are good teachers. What did you learn?"

"All I could think about for forty days was bread. All I felt was loneliness and shame that my life was going nowhere. I almost didn't come out, I was so ashamed. I discovered I was ordinary. Utterly not special. I knew what it was to need help. It's a small thing to know, but it's amazing how it changes you.

"I could recognize hunger. I could see it in people at the sides of the street. And I knew loneliness. I can't walk by it anymore now that I know it intimately. That old woman sitting in the sun? The beggar at the crossroads? The leper? The child with no one to play with? I know their loneliness in mine.

"I gave away what I had on the way home.

"People treated me like a fool. But I wasn't. I was less than a fool. I was nothing. I wasn't a great Jewish leader. I wasn't a leader at all. I was a beggar. And I wasn't even Jewish anymore because I no longer felt the need to go to temple. The streets had become my temple.

"I was no longer young or old. Not really. I was whatever was needed. I could tell old stories with the old or play in the dirt with the young. I wasn't even male or female any more.

"I had wanted to lead my people out of Egypt. Saul has slain his thousands; David his tens of thousands. But I am nothing. Someone lost in the desert. And because I give everything away, I am always hungry. I am always in the desert; I am always seeking and never finding God. I am just what I am. What they are."

My mother said, "It's time for you to go. You're ready now."

I didn't know what to say.

I asked, "Can I have a meal before I go?"

She said, "Of course."

She set three places.

We ate.

As I was leaving, I asked, "Will you be all right on your own?"

She said, "Don't be foolish. I've been preparing for this for thirty years."

The Healer

*When Jesus had come down from the mountain, great
crowds followed him; and there was a leper who came
to him and knelt before him, saying, "Lord, if you
choose, you can make me clean." He stretched out his
hand and touched him . . .*

—Matthew 8:1–3

I had never expected to be a healer.

I certainly wasn't prepared.

Not remotely.

John was greater than I could hope to be and he had
never healed. He preached. I would preach, though as of
yet, I didn't know what. My lack of a plan was painfully
clear in my first attempt to preach after emerging from the
desert.

When people talk about that first sermon, there is a great
deal of exaggeration. First of all, it wasn't a mountain; it was
a hill. And it wasn't a complete success by any means.

There were hecklers.

When I said, "Blessed are the poor," there was laughter.
A heckler shouted, "What do you know about poverty?
You're a middle-class carpenter."

THE DIARY OF JESUS CHRIST

When I said that the meek would inherit the earth, there was considerable laughter.

They didn't settle down until I said, "Blessed are those who mourn for they shall be comforted." A woman stood up and said, "Be quiet and let him speak. I lost my husband and I have mourned and it was bitter but slowly a tenderness has returned. God has comforted me."

Things went well from there until I said, "You are the light of the world," and a powerful male voice shouted, "I'm not."

I went on.

"You are the light of the world. A city set on a mountain cannot be hidden. Nor do they light a lamp and then put it under a bushel basket; it is set on a lampstand, where it gives light to all in the house. Just so, your light must shine before others so that they may see your good deeds and glorify your heavenly Father."

So far, so good.

Then I said, "The light of the body is the eye. If your eye is single, your body will be full of light."

A shout came out of the crowd, "Not mine!"

Same voice. I couldn't see the source. Then I saw. We all saw the leper at the edge of the crowd.

"How can you say my body will be full of light?"

I kept speaking. I didn't know what else to do. He said no more.

As we came down the hill, he did not move. In fact, as we began to make a wide circle around him, he approached us. Many stepped back. Assuming that he was begging, I reached into my purse. From a safe distance, I tossed him the coin. He caught it handily, evaluated it with a quick look, and then tossed it back to me.

Shocked, I let the coin fall to the ground.

Thinking he wanted more—and slightly embarrassed I had chosen to give him the smallest coin in my purse—I reached for another but stopped when I heard him speak.

He said in the same powerful voice, "You can heal me."

This surprised me because, as I said, I had never even thought of healing anyone.

He repeated, "I think you can heal me," adding, "if you want to."

If I want to?

If?

At that moment, there was nothing I wished to do more than heal this man.

To my own surprise, I heard myself saying, "Of course I want to."

You must know this was *not* a decision to heal. It was simply an expression of good will. Perhaps even good will tempered with hopelessness. "Of course I want to."

He said, "If you want to, then do it."

To the crowd's horror and over its shouting, we approached one another.

I said, "Let me see your face."

When he dropped his hood, he ceased being a leper. I don't mean he was cured. No. He still bore the deformities of his disease, but he ceased being a bundle of rags at which one tosses a coin to ease one's conscience. I felt shame at the way I had behaved.

He opened his robe enough for me to see the combination of strength and deformity that was his body.

He said, mocking both himself and me, "Tell me, preacher, can this ever be full of light?"

When I touched him, I was not trying to heal him.

I was asking his forgiveness.

In that touch, I felt a shock of intimacy perhaps more profound than I had ever felt outside of sexual union. Perhaps even more intimate.

And still, even then, I was not aware of what was happening.

Only when people fell to their knees and began to praise God, when the leper stripped off his clothing and showed his healthy body, only then did I become aware of the healing.

His body was indeed full of light.

He rushed me before I could object, and then, to my horror, he embraced me with a full body-to-body embrace.

Pushing him from me, I told him harshly to go show himself to the priests. Perhaps they could explain. And I instructed him to tell no one, absolutely no one, what had happened.

He was puzzled by my joyless tone, but, you see, I could not participate in his joy.

I knew immediately and irrevocably that, from his embrace, I had contracted leprosy.

I could not sleep for days. I couldn't stop washing my hands, my head, everything.

I knew I could never be with people again.

I prayed. I vowed to God that I would never touch a sick person again if he would let me get away with this one time.

I vowed I would do what the law required and I set about doing it.

For my situation, Leviticus calls for a ceremonial cleansing performed away from any gathering of people.

It requires two live clean birds, cedar wood, scarlet yarn, and hyssop. One of the birds is to be killed over fresh water in a clay pot; the live bird must then be dipped seven times into the blood of the bird that was killed. On the seventh day, you must shave off all your hair—head, beard, eyebrows. Two male lambs must be presented to the Lord and sacrificed in the sanctuary. The priest is then to take some of the blood of the offering and put it on the lobe of the right ear, on the thumb of the right hand and on the big toe of the right foot.

On the sixth day, as I began to shave off my eyebrows—the first one was gone—a priest from the temple approached me in the field.

I warned him to stay away but he approached.

He was the priest to whom the leper had presented himself.

When I asked him if I was performing the ritual correctly, he paused before saying that I was indeed performing the ritual as required. And it was his experience that this helped truly ill people but, in my case, he thought the ritual would be useless.

"Jewish law," he said, "preoccupied as it is with cleanliness and health, is good for hypochondriacs. In fact, it creates them."

I knew then that he did not understand my predicament. How could he? He had never cured a leper.

Before I could despair completely, he said, "You're a friend of Magdalene, aren't you?" I said I was. He knew her well and suggested I consult with her. Then he left me.

I freed the remaining bird and abandoned the rites half done.

As I approached her dwelling, I shouted, "Unclean! Unclean!"

Magdalene, drying her hands, came out to greet me, saying, "Shouting "Unclean" at me is a waste of both of our time."

Magdalene, a healer, was considered unclean because she turned away no one who was ill, no matter what the disease. She welcomed all. Those she could not cure, she comforted. For her pains, she was considered unclean.

She asked me what happened to my eyebrow.

I told her the entire story.

She responded by saying, "And because the leper was healed, you feel you must be sick?"

I nodded.

She said, "I'm not sure it works that way."

She told me to come around back where there was an enclosed area with a washstand and a basin. Next to it were ewers of water and oil. She told me to wash myself completely in the water and perfumed oil.

Which I did.

As I was washing, she came in, sat and watched. I asked what she was doing. She said, "What you did for the leper. Looking at you. Seeing you."

She sat. She watched. I washed.

I felt all my imperfections. All the things I would change about my body. My body had not yet recovered from my fasting in the desert.

I said, "It's hard to be looked at."

She nodded and said, "Imagine what it was like for the leper."

She continued, "I don't know much about miracles but I do know a great deal about healing. I think it might have been as much your look as your touch that healed him."

I washed and let myself be seen.

I felt no judgment.

Over time, my body relaxed.

My fear vanished.

Slowly, my body filled with light.

As I dried myself, I asked her why we don't look on one another this way always.

She said, "I do."

As she left, she said under her breath, "Men."

This was the first time that Magdalene returned me to life.

Under the Fig Tree

The next day Jesus decided to go to Galilee. He found
Philip and said to him, "Follow me." Now Philip was
from Bethsaida, the city of Andrew and Peter. Philip
found Nathanael and said to him, "We have found him
about whom Moses in the law and also the prophets
wrote, Jesus son of Joseph from Nazareth." Nathanael
said to him, "Can anything good come out of Nazareth?"
Philip said to him, "Come and see." When Jesus saw
Nathanael coming toward him, he said of him, "Here is
truly an Israelite in whom there is no deceit!" Nathanael
asked him, "Where did you get to know me?" Jesus
answered, "I saw you under the fig tree before Philip
called you." Nathanael replied, "Rabbi, you are the Son
of God! You are the King of Israel!" Jesus answered, "Do
you believe because I told you that I saw you under the
fig tree? You will see greater things than these."
—John 1:43–50

When Nathaniel asked, "Can anything good come out of
Nazareth?" I don't know why, but it *bothered* me. I grew up
in Nazareth. Nazareth is my home. So I found myself saying,
"Do you always say exactly what's on your mind? No guile?
No filter?"

Nathaniel, self-satisfied, smiled and nodded, clearly dis-
missing this Nazarene.

I said, "Care to apologize?"

He challenged me. "Name me *one* good thing that's ever
come out of Nazareth, and I will."

I thought, "Enough of this!"

I said, "I don't have time for this. I'm on the way to a
wedding and my mother will kill me if I don't get there on
time, but I want you to know something."

"What?" he asked.

I took my time.

Then I whispered, "I *saw* you. Under the fig tree."

That took the smile off his face.

He said quietly, "What?"

I leaned in.

"I ... saw you ... under ... the fig tree."

He stuttered, "What...what did you see?"

I walked away.

He stood there dumbfound.

Then he shouted after me, *"I wasn't doing anything."*

I shouted over my shoulder, "Fine. I have to be in Cana.
If you'll excuse me ..."

He shouted back, "Wait a minute," and ran to catch up
with me and the group.

He had no desire to be with us but fell into step with the
group. He kept trying to find a time to speak with me alone,
but the others kept milling about me, talking, laughing,
singing. After a while, he walked next to me and said quietly,
"You have to understand. We weren't doing anything
wrong."

I said, "We? Hmmm. An hour ago it was only you. And
you said you weren't doing anything at all. Which is it?"

I walked faster, leaving him standing still.

He wanted to go back, but he couldn't leave this unfinished business. I shouted over my shoulder, "You're invited to the wedding. These fools are all crashing it. One more won't make much of a difference."

He ran to catch up.

Then, the wedding. The wine. You know the story.

As the evening wore on, I was a little drunk and sitting by myself when Nathaniel, looking worn down, sat down opposite me.

I said, "It used to be I went to weddings of people my own age. Now I'm thirty and everybody getting married is ten years younger than me. I think it might be over for me and weddings."

Nathaniel said, "Me too."

I said, "You're still a young man."

He said, "You saw me under the fig tree. Weddings are not for me ... Will you turn me in?"

I said, "To whom? For what?"

He said, "The temple. My family. My family would turn its back on me. What I am is a sin."

I said, "I have you dead to rights, you know. It's against the law. You should be stoned to death."

He said, "No one believes that anymore."

I said, "You do."

He nodded.

We sat in silence.

I said, "You *know* the penalties—even the death penalty—and *still* you go."

Looking away, he nodded.

I said, "You must be very brave."

He looked back at me, surprised.

"Brave?" he said. "No one has ever called me that."

We looked at one another.

I said, "Dance with me, Nathaniel."

He said, "You're crazy."

I said, "It's a wedding. No one will care. Besides, I brought the wine. No one will say anything."

We danced.

Nathaniel is a good dancer.

People applauded us.

As we danced, we talked.

I said, "You know, I was in the monastery for a while."

He nodded. "Qumran."

I said, "Yes, purest place in the world. We were so pure our skin bled from ritual washing, from washing and bleached cloth. Somehow that was supposed to bring us to God. Perhaps for some it did."

"Not for you?"

I shook my head.

"I'll tell you what I saw under the fig tree..."

He waited.

"I saw tenderness...I saw affection...You tell me...did I see love?"

He nodded.

I said, "The old law is passing away. There will be a new law. And you know what? It will be harder than the old law because the new law is love."

He just kept looking at me.

I said looking around us, "These men, these men who follow me? They are good men. Hard-working men. But..."

I looked at Nathaniel.

"But none of them—not one—has ever risked his life for love."

I looked to see if he understood what I was saying.

He did. He truly did.

Before the tears could fall, Nathaniel dropped to his knees right there on the dance floor. He took my hands and said, "If they're right, if you *are* the Messiah? That would be fine with me."

I said, "You really don't have any filters, do you?"

He shook his head and said, "You are the son of God."

I asked, "I am? You're sure of that?"

He said, "On my life, you are the son of God."

"So, if I'm the son of God..."

"Yes?" he asked.

I said, "Would you be willing to revise your opinion of Nazareth?"

Cana

On the third day there was a wedding in Cana of
Galilee, and the mother of Jesus was there. Jesus and his
disciples had also been invited to the wedding. When the
wine gave out, the mother of Jesus said to him, "They
have no wine."

John 2:1–3

The important thing to remember is that my mother is perfect.

You would think this would make things easier, but it never did.

Perfect people do not have a great deal of patience with those who are less perfect. For her, the cup is always half empty, as it is for all perfect people.

When I was younger, I didn't care much about perfection. This could annoy her, not that she could show it because that would be less than perfect. She behaved her annoyance, which is the essence of being passive aggressive. Which she was. She had high expectations. If something was less than perfect, she expected you to do something about it, and sooner rather than later. And turning up at a wedding feast with twelve guests, as I did, was considerably less than perfect.

So, when the wine ran out, she expected me to do something about it.

Not that running out of wine would have bothered my mother—she didn't drink—but the situation bothered her, and she expected me to fix it.

It's important that you know that, to this point, nothing miraculous had ever happened to me, so a miracle was not what she or I was expecting. What my mother was expecting was fruit punch which, frankly, would have pleased her more than wine because she didn't like drunkenness.

And it didn't look that hard. The wedding was in an orchard. There was lots of fruit and cloves and sugar, so that's what I set about organizing.

My first hint that anything had gone wrong was when an old man who hadn't spoken to his wife in years stood up and sang her a love song. Beautifully. So beautifully that we all stopped and listened.

When he finished, he held up his cup to toast his wife.

The headwaiter took the cup from his hand, smelled it, spun the wine in the glass, smelled it again and called for a glass for himself.

He sipped it and tried to describe it.

He said it tasted to him like liquid night, like sap from a tree of the Garden of Eden, like liquid gold. And this from a man who approved of very few wines.

People began to drink and odd things began to happen.

The families of the bride and groom who had been avoiding one another during the party because each felt that their child had married beneath them began to speak to one another.

They discovered mutual acquaintances.

They began to laugh.

They began to compliment the other's child, praising beauty they had overlooked before.

The rabbi began to tell off-color jokes that were actually very funny.

The band, which was not very good, began to sound better to everyone.

The volume level went up and people from the town who had come to complain about the noise were offered wine. They joined the party, and the decibel level notched itself up.

There was plenty of wine.

One hundred and eighty gallons of the most wonderful wine anyone had ever tasted.

Fights broke out.

The people who were getting into fights were enjoying the fighting.

There were political and religious fights for the older ones and fist fights for the younger in which no one got hurt too badly. Little children ran between the tables and there was dancing and laughter and romance in the dark corners and embracing and I thought, "Oh, so this is what the kingdom of God looks like—glorious chaos and a deep underlying confidence that everything will turn out all right." More people joined in and the party got a second and a third wind with the musicians playing with passion and everyone dancing when suddenly everything was brought to a halt by a voice.

Someone was singing.

We all turned to look.

It was my mother.

She was standing on a table.

She was holding a glass of wine.

Half empty.

Someone refilled it and she drank.

Then, with everyone looking on, she sang sweetly but powerfully a song I had heard before many times.

My soul glorifies the lord and my spirit rejoices in God my savior. For she that is mighty has done great things for me—holy is her name.

And everybody sang, "*Holy is her name.*"

And she was beautiful.

You don't usually notice your mother's beauty, but I was stunned by hers and I could see for a moment what she must have looked like thirty years ago before I was born and I regretted that I had not known her then.

Her song brought shape to the chaos and everyone formed a single circle, joining in a spinning dance around my mother, who was spinning in the opposite direction on a table.

And we sang and danced until dawn when the bride and groom emerged from the house.

No one had noticed them leave the party.

And, fresh from the marriage bed, they were beautiful in a new way that made us feel contented in our bodies—proud of them no matter what they looked like. They were us, after all, and we were staggeringly beautiful.

We made them breakfast and drank the last of the wine.

Of course, the next day my mother denied that she had ever gotten up on a table to sing, but she did and everybody saw it.

As we left, people said, "We must do this again some time."

I thought, "Again? We must do this always."

And from that morning on, we did.

Cousins

Then there appeared to him an angel of the Lord, standing at the right side of the altar of incense. When Zechariah saw him, he was terrified, and fear overwhelmed him. But the angel said to him, "Do not be afraid, Zechariah, for your prayer has been heard. Your wife Elizabeth will bear you a son, and you will name him John.

—Luke 1:11–13

Angels were involved in John's conception. I always felt this skewed his sense of human reproduction. When he was told the facts of life by other children, he accepted the facts but felt they were incomplete. "What about the angel?" he would ask.

There were angels involved in my birth as well, but my parents wisely had kept that from me until the fundamentals were in place.

One day at the Jordan, while John was taking a break from setting the world on fire, I asked him, "John, do you miss having sex like other people?"

He said, "I don't think about it much. I took a vow not to know women, you know."

I asked, "Why?"

He said, "I've done a lot of foolish things. Not so much the honey and locusts. Locusts are very tasty and who doesn't like honey? But the long hair? Living in the wild? Absurd. The vow is just one more absurdity. I don't know why."

Nonsense. John did nothing without purpose. But you couldn't force him to tell you anything, so I waited.

"Sex, cousin," he said finally, "sex is a stunning force. It is in and under and around everything. It will allow nothing to get in its way. It does glorious and terrible things. You know what sex is?"

I asked to hear his version.

"Sex is life's desire to go on."

I waited. He went on.

"That's not what I have. That's what I am.

"But this desire? It isn't only for me to go on. Or my line. It's for all of us. If I see someone blind, I want to give them sight. If I see someone lame, I want to make them walk. When I see someone who can walk, I want to make them fly. God help me, when I see someone die, I want to bring them back to life."

I asked, "Have you ever tried to do these things?"

He shook his head.

"They are beyond me. These are loving acts and I am fundamentally a violent person. Sometimes I think all I am is desire. It fills me so much sometimes that I can't breathe. Sometimes what I am scares me. Have you noticed how much I shout? The only safe place for me really is the desert. There are things I would like to do—gentle things, healing things—but the violence gets in the way. Violence will be the end of me."

He could tell I was not satisfied with his answer.

He smiled and threw his arm over my shoulder. "You're different, little one. You don't have to concern yourself with sex."

"No?"

"No."

"Why not?"

He smiled and said, "You're an angel."

I tried to explain to him that my time in the desert had taught me that I was the opposite of an angel. Starved, I was voracious. Lonely, I was lustful. Desiring to be nothing but spirit, I was only my body.

He laughed as he said, "It was a great mistake for you to go into the desert. Some people it helps. Not you. You are not a creature of the desert. You are a city boy. You weep over the beauty of the city. Go to the city. Fill it with love. Make it glow from within. Believe me, all humankind shall see the salvation of God."

I asked, "How can you be so confident that God will come bringing salvation for the world?"

He answered with a smile, "It's already here, little one."

"Where, John, where?"

"You can't see it, little one, from where you are sitting."

"Where is it?" I asked.

He laughed and said, "I'm looking at it, cousin. It's you. You are salvation for the world. It couldn't be plainer."

I said, "I wish I had your conviction."

He said, "Can you at least ask the question? Could it be you? Promise me you will ask."

I said, "I can deny you nothing. But I am not an angel. I need to eat. I need wine. Lots of wine. I need companions. I need to hold and be held."

He said, "Good. I'm tired and sore. Hold me and let me rest."

He put his head in my lap and slept.

As he slept, I spoke into his ear when he could not hear, "I have made a leper clean, John. What I am scares me, John."

Without opening his eyes, John smiled and said, "Well, look at that. I made a blind man see."

Give a Child a Scorpion

*Is there anyone among you who, if your child asks for a
fish, will give a snake instead of a fish? Or if the child
asks for an egg, will give a scorpion?*

—Luke 11:11–12

He sat alone after the sermon.

When I'd seen him in the crowd before, I would find myself preaching to him. His quality of listening made it possible
for me to articulate what I was thinking. The questions in his
eyes guided me. He had very expressive eyes. But today, I
could tell I was losing him. More than that, I was offending
him.

Simply to keep speaking, I had to shift my focus to others and, when it was all done and I was mobbed with con-
gratulations on my brilliant sermon, I saw him sitting alone
and at some distance.

I wondered if I should leave my admirers and approach
him. I like praise as much as the next, but I knew it would be
cowardly to ignore a critic. I went to him, but I hedged my
bets. I tried to make my failure his problem. I asked sympa-
thetically, "Are you unwell?"

"Go away," he barked.

I said, "Look, I'm sorry if I offended you. It wasn't my intention. I've seen you in the crowd before. You usually like what I have to say."

He nodded sadly, looked up at me and said, "I thought you might be the one. . . . You are a disappointment."

I agreed, "To no one more than myself. But help me," I said. "What did I say that upset you?"

"You didn't upset me. Don't make this my problem."

He was on to me.

"You were wrong."

What was left but to invite his honest critique?

"Very well, then. How was I wrong?"

He said with burning, quiet anger, "How dare you? How dare you call God a father? The scriptures do not support you. God is not a father to Abraham, to Isaac, to Jacob. He is not a father to Moses. Yes, father is mentioned in the scriptures but only seven times and seven is nothing compared to the times he is called creator, warrior, and lawgiver. He is a burning bush, a pillar of fire, a refiner's fire, a punisher, an oven in which the wicked are burnt to ash." Anger made him articulate. We had that in common.

"What can I say?" I said. "A father? Well, we all know a father's love . . ."

"Do we? Do we? How arrogant you are. How unthinking," he said. "'What father will hand his son a snake when he asks for bread? A scorpion when he asks for an egg?' *There . . . are . . . such . . . fathers.*"

His cheeks were red with anger and embarrassment at having said too much, but he couldn't stop himself.

"'Ask and you shall receive?' Maybe. But what if there is no one to ask?"

I could feel the size of his wound, a wound I had not intended to open. I could feel it being larger than his body could contain. Perhaps larger than the world.

I had sudden clarity on one thing.

I knew that this young man, radiant with pain, was a hole in the heart of God. If I could not bring him to God's heart, my life would have no purpose.

He said, "I like the law. I love it. I embrace it; this law that you are trying to get rid of. You obey the law—all 613 of the commandments. The law keeps you safe. God will not notice you. He only notices you when you fail him."

"That is a hard god."

"Shame on you for making him harder. By making God a father, you deprive me of any god at all. Your god doesn't exist for me."

I sat next to him, grateful he didn't move away.

"Well, it's an image," I said, drawing in the dirt with my fingers. "God is greater than any image."

I looked for another image.

"What about mother? Can you imagine God as a mother?"

That caught his attention.

He said, "Can you?"

I said, "Actually, the story about pounding on a locked door is a story about my mother. She could be relentless. Never for herself. But as an advocate for me? Or the poor? Whew! Once I asked her, 'Do you ever think that God might be a woman?'"

She said, "Please don't bother me with idle talk. I have things to do."

"But I pressed her. 'No, really. Could God be a woman?'"

She said as she cleaned, "Look at the state the world is in and tell me you think a woman could have left it like an unmade bed. If God went through what we go through, if God had to carry life within him for the better part of a year, he would be more careful with how he treats it."

He nodded sadly. But sadness was better than anger.

"My mother would agree with yours. If you asked her for anything and she could give it to you, she would. But she's gone now. If I go to my house and knock, there will be no answer. If I ask, it will not be given."

We sat in silence for a minute.

Then I said, "You haven't asked me."

"For what?" he said.

"A fish. An egg."

"I don't want a fish," he said. "I don't want an egg."

"Ask. Ask me anything. I will give it to you."

"I have learned to do things on my own. I don't ask."

"Fine. Don't," I said.

I took out my coin purse, emptied it and divided the coins in half.

"Here is my money," I said. "Half of it is yours."

I opened his hand and put half of my silver coins in it.

He looked at me confused.

"Not enough? You drive a hard bargain. Here is all of it."

I put the rest of the silver in his hand.

"Here. You can have the purse as well," and I gave him the purse.

He said, "Are you mocking me?"

I took off my sandals and put them in front of him.

"Here are my sandals. They're good sandals. Very few miles on them. Shall I put them on your feet for you?"

I removed his old sandals and put my new ones on his feet.

He was puzzled, but I could tell he liked the sandals.

"Ask *anything* and I will give it to you. Any time. Day or night. If I have it, it is yours."

He smiled at me for the first time.

An embarrassed smile.

An unbelieving smile.

But a smile.

"You're insane," he said.

"OK, then. If you insist. Here is my tunic."

I took it off and, standing in my loincloth, I held it out to him.

Now he was laughing, genuinely laughing.

When I went to remove my loincloth, he said, "Stop there." He said. "Stop there before you embarrass us all."

He was looking at me the way he looked at me when I preached. He looked hungry for my words. My thoughts became clear, and with clarity came feeling.

"What can I give you that will assure you of my love?"

He had no answer.

"I am not your father, but I feel a father's love for you. And I tell you, if I were your father, I would be the proudest man in the world."

He said quietly and hoarsely, "I'm not used to such praise."

"What's your name, wounded one?"

He looked up at me. He looked younger as his face relaxed into a kind of peace with itself. "Actually, my name means praise. Praise be to God. That's what they named me."

I nodded.

"Your name is Judas, then?"

He nodded.

"Judas, come with us. I will do what it takes to convince you that God loves you with a father's love."

He exploded, "Haven't you been listening? I don't want a father's love."

"Well," I said backing off, "then mine will have to do."

But would it?

If not, I should have left him alone rather than open a wound I couldn't heal.

Better I should not have been born.

The Chosen and Not

He went up the mountain and called to him those
whom he wanted, and they came to him.

—Mark 3:13

All in all, I thought it went very well. I mean, there were not
unlimited choices.

Not many people would be willing to uproot themselves
from their lives to follow me, but I was pleased with us as a
group. And the men were very happy to have been chosen;
giddy even. I don't think they had ever been chosen for anything before. I was asking them to be itinerant and homeless,
and they were behaving as if they had just won the prize of
a lifetime.

I had discussed all the men with Magdalene at length.

She knew men. She understood men. And she knew that
developing a core group of good men was important. We
talked until we had a consensus on all but two. She felt that
Judas and Peter were both questionable choices, capable of
betrayal as much as loyalty. All in all, she thought they were
the best of a bad lot.

After the announcement, I asked her if she was happy with
how it went. She answered with surprising coldness, "That's
not the question. You have to live with them. Are you happy?"

THE DIARY OF JESUS CHRIST

I told her that by-and-large, all-in-all, given-the-options, taking-everything-into-account, yes, I was happy.

She said, "Well, good on you," turned her back, and walked away, leaving me puzzled.

I shouted after her, "Let's celebrate tonight. Let's have a party."

Without turning back to look, she said, "Fine. Who are you going to get to cook?"

As she walked away, a chasm opened at my feet. A shadow passed over my heart. I had hurt her somehow. I had not intended to, but I had.

And I didn't know how.

Our food that night was simple. And when I say simple, I mean fisherman-simple. Peter and Andrew cooked. Fish. We ate endless fish in the early days. The women usually made something special out of them, but Peter and Andrew cooked like fishermen. They gutted the fish, put them on the fire, took them out of the fire, and we ate them.

Even so, the men had a genuinely good time.

They rejoiced in one another's company.

They loved being the chosen ones. They gloried in it. They said to me, "Look, we know we aren't what you were looking for. We aren't scholars. We can't quote Torah. But we can tell, by having been chosen, one thing. We know how much you love us."

And this broke my heart, because it was true.

And I knew now how I had hurt Magdalene.

The women ate in a group by themselves that night, which was not unusual.

As I approached, I heard their laughter.

I heard it stop as I arrived.

"Do you mind if I join you?"

The women looked at Magdalene; she did not look up from her meal.

"Of course you're welcome." she said. "We exclude no one from our circle."

As I sat and ate, the women laughed at the look on my face.

"Is this...is this *really* the same fish that the men are eating?"

They had prepared it with lemon and saffron. It was hard to believe it was actually the same fish. Magdalene was accepting no compliments.

I complimented them on the wine.

Magdalene said, "Joanna brought it from Herod's palace where her husband works."

I said, "It's very good."

Magdalene said, "Yes. It's what you have been drinking for weeks."

We fell into a silence.

I said, "You are angry with me."

The silence deepened.

I asked, "Are you angry with me for not choosing you?"

The women faded away quietly into the night.

When they were gone, I said, "But we discussed all the choices and you never said a word."

Magdalene said, "I am angry that it didn't cross your mind. And, to be fair, I am angry that it didn't cross mine."

I asked, "Can we talk about it?"

She said, "I'm not sure that we can even talk at all."

Then she stood and faded into the night.

Alone by the fire, I thought I should fade into the night as well. And I did. As soon as I had finished eating the fish.

I looked for her first thing the next morning.

I was up before the men, and she was up before most of the women.

"I didn't sleep last night. You?"

She shook her head and said, "I was wrong to criticize you last night."

I said, "You didn't say a word against me. That's worse." I said, "Say what you need to say."

She asked, "Are you sure you want to hear it?"

I said, "Frankly, I'm grateful that you're speaking to me at all...I don't understand the problem. We discussed this endlessly. I just did what we had agreed on doing."

She said, "Yes, we had discussed who would be in the inner circle. Yes, we went over the names. It never occurred to me—and this is on me—it never occurred to me that I wanted to be in that group. Never. Until you started to read the names. Then, as the names were called, I found myself waiting to hear my name. When all the names were called, you said these are the ones I want. Seeing the joy, the rapture, the delight of those being called, I suddenly felt something I had never felt with you. Un-chosen. Omitted. Passed over."

I said, "But you are more dear to me than any of them. You are the one I sought advice from in choosing them."

She said, "What can I say? You aren't like the priests in the temple. When you said 'Blessed are the poor,' you didn't say 'Blessed are poor *men.*' When you said 'Blessed are the meek,' you didn't say, 'Blessed are meek *men.*' I had always felt included until that moment."

We were silent. There was nothing to say.

She went on, "But I looked at them—the inner circle—and I know them. I know them better than they know themselves. I know what men are. How they pretend to be brave in confronting other men who pretend to be brave. They are like dogs barking at one another in the street. I know how far they can be trusted and I can tell you this. They will *not* be there for you at the end. And we both know there is only one ending. I know the men of the temple. Many of them I know very well. I know how brittle their self-confidence is—and you are challenging everything they believe in. The ending will not be good. And those men you chose? They won't be there for you in the end."

Her words were sharp and clear and cut deeply into both of us.

She finished, "And I will be."

I said, "Maybe it won't end badly."

She said, "Please. We know one another too well for lying."

I noticed she had not packed.

"So," I said, "You're not coming with us?"

"Not this time. Not on this journey.

"But I will be here when you get back and we will see then. I have to adjust. I have to find out what I am in this new world. I have to understand how I love you. I haven't loved you as a wife loves. Or as a lover. I think...I think I have loved you as if you were my sister. Eye to eye. As my equal. And I have to think about that now."

I said, "You know men. What am I thinking?"

She said, "I never have a clue about you."

I said, "I am thinking I will miss you as I would miss my soul. My soul left me last night when you walked away. You have returned to me now. And..."

"And?" she said.

"And, as for the ending, if it comes, I will be there for you as well."

She said, "Death ends all."

I said, "Even if it comes to that, even if it comes to death, I will find you. I will be there for you. On my life."

She said, "On my life as well."

We kissed and we left one another.

For a time.

She went away by herself.

And I went away with those I had chosen.

Walking Away

*Then the scribe said to him, "You are right, Teacher; you
have truly said that 'he is one, and besides him there is
no other'; and 'to love him with all the heart, and with
all the understanding, and with all the strength,' and 'to
love one's neighbor as oneself,'—this is much more
important than all whole burnt offerings and sacrifices."
When Jesus saw that he answered wisely, he said to him,
"You are not far from the kingdom of God."*
—Mark 12:32–34

I apologized later.

I'm just so used to having scribes trying to trap me, I assumed he was one more. So, when he asked me to reduce
the entire law to two commandments, I found myself shouting at him, "LOVE! Damn it! LOVE GOD AND LOVE YOUR
NEIGHBOR!"

So it took my breath away when he came back with,
"Well said, teacher! That's exactly right! Love is greater than
the law! Love is the law!"

I didn't see that coming. That was a first from the scribes.
But what moved me more than being agreed with was what
he called me. He called me teacher. Twice my age, he'd

THE DIARY OF JESUS CHRIST

been working in the temple all his adult life and he called me teacher.

I apologized for shouting at him.

He said, "Apologize for nothing, teacher. At least not to me. I have been waiting for you my whole life. I loved you even before I knew you."

He loved me, even in the face of my shouting. I had treated him as an enemy and his love did not flinch. He was practicing what I preached.

I am almost embarrassed to say this, but his love for me thrilled me the way love always does. Unsettled me. And I had done no miracle for him.

I said, "You know, you've made a mistake."

He said, "No, I haven't."

And I said, "No, not about me. About you. You said love is greater than the law. When your brother scribes at the temple hear about this, they will not welcome you back. You will lose your job."

"Lose my job!" he said. "Thank God! Lose my job? What a pleasure!"

I said, "Really? Are you ready to walk away from that? Taking care of the temple has been your life."

He said, "Who needs a job when the Messiah comes? Though I warn you, not everyone will be as pleased as I am to lose my job. Some will see the coming of the Messiah as a terrible interruption of religious services. Better to walk away. We are always walking away. Abraham walked away from an old life to start a new one. And he was eighty. I am only sixty."

"Only?" I said.

"Only! I am ready to walk away. We are a walk-away people. We walked away from slavery in Egypt to the unknown Sinai. We walked into exile and walked back with poetry flowing from us. We are always walking away. What have you walked away from?"

"Well," I said, "Not as much as you. I did walk away from a secure job."

He said, "Two of a kind! You have said so much that has been in my heart. If I understand you..."

And he proceeded to explain me to myself.

"What's human is divine?"

I nodded.

"And mercy is justice?"

He couldn't be stopped.

"And there is a chosen people and it is everyone!"

He shouted the last statement to everyone.

"Have I understood you?"

I said, "What an excellent scribe you must be!" Laughing, I said, "You are walking faster than I am. Slow down, old man."

"You know," he said. "Teacher. Son. Brother. Christ. I don't feel like an old man. I feel young. I feel young and in love."

"That's good," I said, "because I am feeling old, very old. I feel like I am living my life in dog years. Every one year is seven. That's how old I feel. At 30 I feel 210!"

"Oh," he said, "you are much older than that. You are living in God-years, and every day is an eternity. Every hour. Every second.

"Be still. Let me take care of you now as I have taken care of the temple.

"Let me polish you up. Let me kiss your hands and wash your feet.

"Let me polish you to a shine.

"Let's sit in one another's arms and let the scribes call us outlaws and criminals.

"Let's worship God within one another.

"Yes, you be my temple and let me be yours for an hour, a moment, an eternity."

I said, "You know, you are not far from the kingdom."

He said, "Close! I don't want to be close to the kingdom. I want to be in the kingdom. I love you and you love me and that is the kingdom. That's the secret, isn't it? We are the temple. The people, they are the temple. Enter them and you enter the kingdom. Have I understood you? And now I have to apologize to you."

I echoed him. "Never apologize to me, brother, teacher, friend, if I may call you friend."

He wouldn't be denied his confession. "I brought you here. I prayed you into being. I asked God for you and now you're here. My fault." And then, most confidentially, "And I know how much you're are going to have to walk away from."

I didn't want to spoil the moment, so I said, "Do I have to do all that today?"

And he said, "No."

I said, "Be with me in the kingdom today and we will let tomorrow take care of tomorrow."

And he said, "Amen! And do not worry, my friend. Once people understand you as I do, who will be able to resist the joy of walking with you? Who? It will be a parade!"

And we took a walk.

Take Nothing for the Journey

*He called the twelve and began to send them out two by
two, and gave them authority over the unclean spirits.
He ordered them to take nothing for their journey except
a staff; no bread, no bag, no money in their belts; but to
wear sandals and not to put on two tunics.*

—Mark 6:7–9

The truth is, I sent them away because I had had it with
them up to here. They were making me crazy. Despite the
fact that I was teaching them every day, they knew nothing.
Nothing. In fact, every day, they seemed to know less. So I
said, "Go. Go out into the world. See how hard it is to try
to change it."

What I actually meant was that I needed time to myself
to evaluate how far I had come and I could not do that while
constantly instructing them and breaking up their fights.

The morning they were setting out, you should have
seen them. They were so loaded down with baggage they
could barely move: luggage, walking sticks, a tent, ham-
mocks, money pouches, food for a week, two weeks, wine,
water, bread, knives. Knives!

"Knives?" I said. "You're taking knives?"

Thomas flashed a huge knife and smiled. "Robbers, beware!" he said. Matthew said, "It's dangerous out there. You don't understand that. You grew up in a family business. I was out in the world. So were the fishermen. You have to be prepared."

I said, "Yes, but you look like peddlers with your store on your back. You look like a caravan without camels. Put it all down. Get rid of it. It's not going to help you."

"Not a chance," Thomas said.

"Look," I said. "When I was in the desert..."

They rolled their eyes. "Not the desert again."

"When I was in the desert, I was scared, too. I took along provisions. I had a knife at my side.

"I saw animals. I saw jackals, mountain lions. I was terrified.

"But you can only be frightened for so long before something snaps. Once I stopped being terrified, I began to see the beauty of the fierceness of the world. The animals were perfect and, yes, they could harm me and I was frightened.

"I saw bones on the floor of the desert and there was beauty in death, too, and if that's what God had in mind for me, let me have that beauty as well. That's when I first felt God rising up within me.

"I knelt down and wept and felt an emptiness inside me.

"That's what I have been trying to teach you ever since. Give up everything and allow space for God to rise."

They nodded and said, "See you in a month then."

They waved and off they went, jangling and clanging, money chinking in their pockets, wares clattering on their backs, wine sloshing in their wine skins.

I was glad to see the back of them. They understood nothing and, who knows, maybe now that they were gone, I could start to feel God's presence again.

When they came back a month later, they had nothing. Nothing at all. They had lost weight. Their faces had new, truer contours.

And, remarkably, they were silent.

I asked, "What happened? Were you robbed?"

The first one to speak was Matthew. He said, "Damn you, Joshua. I couldn't get your words out of my head."

"You were generous?" I asked.

"Against my will. It's hard to travel carrying all of the paraphernalia I had, so I gave away an extra coat. It lightened the load."

Nathaniel said, "And how can you pass hungry people when you have extra food in your pack? So I gave away food."

Andrew said, "Me too. And the more I gave away, the lighter the load became."

Peter said, "The more I gave away, the more people said good things about me. That was new. They said, 'Look. There goes a generous man.' It made me feel good." Then his voice tightened. "But after a while, I had less and less. I became frightened."

Thomas said, "Me, too. And it finally happened. As I was walking from one town to another one, robbers suddenly surrounded me. The last thing, the *last* thing I had, was my knife. So I said, 'Look. I have nothing except this." I drew my knife and it flashed in the moonlight. They all jumped back. Then I turned it around so the handle faced them. I said, 'This knife? It's a good one. Better than yours. So, if you are planning to slit my throat, do it properly and use this.'"

We waited.

Thomas said, "They had no idea of what to make of me, so they said, 'Let's bring this fool home and feed him and see if he regains his wits. And take that knife away from him be-fore he hurts somebody with it.'"

The others nodded, indicating that something like that had happened to them too.

Peter said, "After a while they stopped saying, 'Look at the generous man' and started saying, 'Look at him. He has nothing. Let's feed him.'"

All of them agreed. "Around the fires, in homes, by the roadside, we heard stories. Some beautiful; many sad. Of loss. Of sickness. Of loneliness. The things we all have in common."

They fell silent. They exchanged looks but said nothing. So I asked, "What?"

John spoke for the group when he said, "What did it feel like when you touched the leper and cured him? Were you surprised?"

"Well," I said, "I was mostly surprised that I touched him. After that, things seemed to move along on their own."

They all nodded.

John said, "When I finally had nothing—even my sandals were gone—I could feel the pain of the folks around me echo inside me until it became a cry to God. Yes, like the howl of a jackal in the desert."

I asked, "What happened then?"

They all looked at John.

John said, "Then the miracles began."

Peter said, "We started to touch people and things began to move along by themselves."

I asked, confident of the answer, "And did you feel God rising up inside you?"

But they all shook their heads no.

Then quietly they began to speak.

James said, "I felt *you*. You within me. I felt your warmth in my touch."

He rested his eyes on me.

Nathaniel said, "I felt your words in my mouth."

He looked up at me.

Peter agreed, "I felt your smile on my lips."

John said, "I felt your presence within me. And then the miracles began."

And, one by one, they moved to their knees and knelt silently in front of me.

Silence.

No one moved.

No one desired to be anywhere but here in this moment.

At first I felt embarrassed.

It requires a certain humility to accept being worshiped.

Bless those moments that prepare you for the work that is to come.

Bless those moments when you know for certain who you are.

Come Follow Me

"When the unclean spirit has gone out of a person, it wanders through waterless regions looking for a resting place, but it finds none. Then it says, 'I will return to my house from which I came.' When it comes, it finds it empty, swept, and put in order. Then it goes and brings along seven other spirits more evil than itself, and they enter and live there; and the last state of that person is worse than the first."

—Matthew 12:43–45

"You have to help me."

A man came up to me. Was he drunk? I couldn't tell. He said, "You have to help me."

I said I would if I could.

He asked, "Can you cast out a demon?"

I said, "Anyone can cast out a demon. You point the finger and say the right words."

He said, "What are the words?"

"It isn't that simple. There isn't a formula. They change from demon to demon. And demons are clever. They're changing their passwords all the time. And that's not the real problem. The real problem is, once they are cast out, what do you do with them? There's no good place to put them. And besides," I said, guessing that his demon was drink, "you can cast out some demons by yourself."

He said, "Oh, this isn't for me."

"Who then?" I asked.

"My wife. My wife is possessed by a demon."

I said, "Be careful of accusing your wife. A house divided against itself cannot stand."

"Oh," he said, "our house fell long ago."

I went to see his wife.

She sat silently in the corner of her darkened house, eyes bright in the darkness.

"What did he say about me?" she asked. "Did he say I was possessed?"

I nodded.

She said, "I'm not possessed. I'm just...sad. No one is interested in me sad. He's interested in me cooking and cleaning. He eats and leaves. We don't talk. No one is interested in me."

I sat and said, "I'm interested."

She said, "Don't bother. I've been sad for so long that even I'm not interested in me. It's like when I was in labor. It went on so long, I even lost interest in giving birth. Or even in my own life. That's how I feel now every day."

I asked, "Where is your child?"

She said, "We had her five years. Now she is no more."

And she wept.

Hours later I came out of the house. There was a crowd around the husband who, by now, was definitely drunk.

He asked, "Well, did you fix her?"

I pointed my finger at him and said, "Evil spirit, be gone."

He said, "*What?*"

I said, "Evil spirit, you will not possess this man."

He said, "Me? Me? I'm not the one possessed by an evil spirit."

His wife appeared at the door, smiling.

He looked at her smile and said, "You did this, didn't you? You told him I was possessed by the devil."

She said, "It's no more than you said about me."

She shouted and pointed at him, "You must be possessed. What else could explain it? You have changed. You have no feeling for me!"

He shouted and pointed at her, "No feeling for *you?* You have no feeling for *me!*"

I said, "If you had no feeling for one another, you wouldn't be standing in the street shouting at one another and I would be home having my dinner."

Then I said to her, "Say it. Speak the word.... Release the demon."

She nodded and spat it out. She said bitterly, "You have no feeling! You do...not...cry!"

He replied, "No. I do not cry. Why do you think I drink? That's why I drink."

"Excuses!" she shouted.

"I'm *scared*, Miriam," he shouted.

She shouted back, "And you think *I'm* not?"

He responded, "No. I am scared of *you.*"

Everyone grew quiet. And grew closer so as not to miss a word.

He said, "I do not feel as *you* feel. There is no bottom to your sorrow. None. I watch the depth of you and I tremble.

Even God can't see to the bottom of your sorrow. I am afraid of *you.*"

This stunned her.

She answered simply, "Don't. Don't be afraid of me. There is nothing to fear in me."

And the first demon departed.

"Go on," I said to her.

She said, "You *blame* me. You blame me for the death of our girl. And I cannot bear that."

And *he* was stunned.

He said, amazed, "Blame? Blame? How?...Never. She was your other self. How could I blame you?"

And the second demon departed.

I said to him, "Find the words."

He said, "I sometimes feel, because I do not cry, that I never loved her. That doubt is killing me."

She couldn't believe what she was hearing.

She couldn't speak.

She looked at the crowd and said, "*Tell him.* All of you. *Tell him* what you know."

And the people in the crowd told him how often they had seen him walking with her on his shoulders...running after her in the street...No other father braided his daughter's hair. And they assured him there was no doubt about his love. Never a doubt. They had all witnessed it time and again.

Another demon was expelled.

And they went on like this for some time, expelling one another's demons. Fighting and shouting and struggling to find the words until all the demons were gone. All seven of them—Fear. Depression. Blame. Rage. Confusion. Hurt. Doubt.

When they were all gone, the man and his wife wept and held one another close. They thanked me and kissed my hands.

I told them this had nothing to do with me. I said, "This is entirely your doing. All I did was point a finger. You found the words."

They invited me to dinner, but I declined.

I said, "I have companions I must see to."

They nodded and respected my wish.

When they went into their house with all their neighbors, I was left standing in the street alone.

Alone.

Except for seven demons.

Seven homeless demons.

They approached me but I pointed my finger at them.

They stepped back.

I said, not for the first time, "Come, follow me."

And they did.

Something I Should Have Done a Long Time Ago

... he then said to the paralytic—"Stand up, take your bed and go to your home." And he stood up and went to his home.

—Matthew 9:6–7

Funny story about a cripple. Not my choice of word. His. Benjamin would insist: he called himself a cripple. "Look at me. Look at the cripple." I would say, "You know, Benji, people would feel more pity for you if you didn't feel so sorry for yourself." And Benji would laugh.

I liked making Benji laugh.

He was the younger brother of Asher, one my best friends growing up. Asher, Benjamin ... the family was set on having an alphabet of children. It was a long time between the first two, so when Benji arrived, the whole village was excited. We couldn't wait for Asher to be a big brother.

But when Ben was born—I was what? Ten?—well, there he was, all scrunched up and not quite right and already beet-red angry. Oh, he was an angry, howling, fierce, little baby. Fierce is the best word, because his happiness was fierce too. Coming off the breast, that child's smile made us laugh. Not all the pieces of Ben worked the way they should, but they worked. And before long, he would be able to scurry across the floor, inventing his own way to move.

Little brothers are a pain, but I liked Asher's little brother. I admired him. I admired his fierceness and the fierceness of the family that circled their wagons around him.

Then something bad happened. Something worse than the crippling effects of whatever it was that had happened to Benjamin in the womb.

We went to Ben's naming at the temple.

Sabbath best clothes.

Asher carrying his brother carefully.

Carefully handing him to the scribe for the ritual of the naming.

The scribe—not a bad man, my teacher as a matter of fact—knew the scriptures inside out. I admired that. I always aimed to impress him and sometimes I did with some tour-de-force recitation of Torah. I was an idiot. A show-off certainly.

He held the baby and we waited for the announcement of the baby's name.

And the scribe, my teacher, spoke out in his resonant voice!

Into the silence of the temple, he shouted, *"Who has sinned that this child has been born this way?"*

There was stunned silence.

Now, his parents were good people, so this accusation made no sense, no matter what the scriptures said.

None of us moved for a long moment.

Then the scribe shouted again, louder this time, *"Who? Who has sinned?"*

Silence.

Footsteps.

Asher walked up to him, took the baby from his arms, handed the child to his parents and attacked my teacher. Asher struck him as hard as a twelve-year-old could. And, as the temple security dragged Asher off the scribe and out of the temple, he screamed at me, "Aren't you going to say something? You know him. He's your teacher. You're his pet. Say something. *Say something!*"

I was ten. What could I say?

My teacher's words put walls between a husband and a wife. Neither suspected the other of sin, so they assumed that they themselves had sinned. They exaggerated their own faults to believe them significant enough for God to so punish them.

And after that, there was no more alphabet of children.

I used to go to the house and sit with Ben and say, "If you don't walk, this will just get worse." He said he had no desire to see anybody in this village. But he loved gossip and collected dirt on everybody. He had a wicked, acid tongue, and he used to make me laugh. I would massage his legs and feel the anger under his laughter. I would scold him sometimes, but he would ask with a smile, "Is that any way to talk to a cripple?"

And now, today, I am returning to my village feeling like a failure.

Yesterday I did an exorcism, and afterward the people thanked me and asked me never to come back because the demon went into their pigs and the pigs went mad. So I am going home. I just want to rest. That's all. Just rest.

But as I approach, there is a crowd. They've heard of what I've been doing and they've turned out to see the prodigal.

And right in the middle of the crowd is Asher and at his feet is Benji on a mattress.

Benji is furious about being exposed to the light.

Benji *never* cries, but tears of shame and rage are rolling down his face. I can tell he's mad at me for causing this even though I had nothing to do with it. I want to say that to him, but, before I can deny responsibility, Asher says three simple things:

"We've heard.

"Do it here.

"Now."

No more needed to be said.

I look at Benji, his face fierce and bright red, and I look up and see my teacher walking down the road toward us. He is the last person I want to see, and I regret ever saying the last shall be first, because here he is.

So, feeling a failure and feeling more failure coming, I kneel down next to Benji and he turns his head away from me.

I say, "Hi, Ben."

He says nothing.

And I say, "Fine. Don't look. But listen. I'm going to say something and it's something very important and you really have to listen."

And Ben barks out, "Why? Why should I listen to you?"

And I say, "Haven't you heard? I'm a holy man now. Everybody knows it. I'm a holy man."

Despite himself, Benji smiles.

I say, "Oh, yes. I'm very holy. In fact...in fact, people are saying I'm a saint."

His smile starts to spread.

"In fact," I say, "people are saying..."

I stand as I say this, "I'm the Messiah."

The word echoes.

People are suddenly quiet.

You can feel the heat rolling off my teacher.

The only sound is Benji laughing.

Benji laughs outright, but I'm not laughing anymore when I say, "What are you laughing about? I am the Messiah. And, as the Messiah..."

I stop until there is silence. And I shout, "As your Messiah, I say something I should have said a very long time ago."

I shout, "Benji, sin had *nothing* to do with it!"

And everybody knows what I am talking about.

And I look at Asher and I say...I say, "Nobody sinned. Nobody. This has *nothing* to do with sin."

Then I look at my teacher and I say, "And God doesn't listen to anyone who says you or your beautiful parents sinned. There is no sin...there is no law...there is no God, if there is no love."

I look into my teacher's eyes and they are flaming. I walk over and I say, "Teacher, I'm sorry, but you're just wrong. And you always have been. I've made allowances, but God has told me you're wrong. You're just wrong, and forgive me for saying this, but I can't say anything else."

My teacher says to me, "I wasted my time with you. You are a blasphemer and you are not welcome in the temple." And his face hardens against me as he walks away.

I hear a voice behind me and I turn to see Benjamin struggling to stand.

It isn't pretty.

He's like a young horse or deer trying to balance on thin, so thin, legs—stick-like legs—and he shouts out to the scribe, "Stop...right...there!"

There is authority in his voice. The scribe stops and turns. And Benji says—shouts, "There is nothing wrong with me. Or my parents. Never has been. And shame on you or anyone who ever thought there was. And you are *not* welcome in my home."

And then, "But the rest of you sinners are. Come with me. It's been too long since we've had a party. We have to celebrate this…this…this pathetic…this blasphemous messiah who's come home to us because he has no place else to go."

And he walked, hobbled, half-fell, half-danced his way away, refusing help from anybody.

I shouted after him, "Benji, get back here and take your bed with you. Don't leave this lying in the street."

And he said, "Really? Is that any way to talk to a cripple?"

Everyone laughed.

And, as the street emptied, the weight of Asher's arm fell over my shoulder. I put my arm over Asher's shoulder though we didn't look at one another. Our eyes were on Benji.

Asher leaned his cheek against my hand.

He kissed my hand and said, "Welcome home."

I said, "That is something I should have done a long time ago."

Asher said, "You really should have. They would have forgiven you then."

Who Will I Love Today?

On one occasion when Jesus was going to the house of a leader of the Pharisees to eat a meal on the sabbath, they were watching him closely. Just then, in front of him, there was a man who had dropsy. And Jesus asked the lawyers and Pharisees, "Is it lawful to cure people on the sabbath, or not?" But they were silent. So Jesus took him and healed him, and sent him away.

—Luke 14:1–4

He didn't seem thankful. That was odd.

Since the leper, cures had been pouring out of me and people had been invariably grateful.

Not this time.

Usually, after I cured, they were kissing my hands and swearing to follow me forever. I'm not in it for the thanks, but even so. I said, "Shouldn't you at least say thank you?"

His name was Nathan and he was an ill-kempt ...what?...sixty? More? He said, "Thank you? For what?"

I said, "For what? For a healing. I only have so many miracles in me and dropsy can be treated with diet and exercise. Cut down on the salt. Okay?"

He said, "Did I *ask* to be cured?"

I said, "Didn't you *want* to be cured?"

"Cured?" he said, "I didn't even know I was *sick*. I just thought I was *old*."

As I walked away, I said, "Well, you're welcome."

He said, "Not so fast. You *used* me."

"*Used* you?"

"You were looking for a fight with the Pharisees and you used me to make your point. Now I have enemies I never had before. And why did you have to cure me on the sabbath? I had dropsy, you say? Then what was the rush? It could have waited. And now I'm on the Pharisees' enemies list! Thanks for nothing!"

I didn't know what to say.

He said, "Look, come to my house tonight and we can fight over dinner. I fight better on a full stomach and in the cool of the evening. My wife is an excellent cook and you look like you could use a good meal. And one meal, it won't give you dropsy."

When I arrived at the house, his wife, Hannah, saw me coming. "So you're the young man who healed my husband against his will. Nothing is simple, is it? I thank you on his behalf."

Nathan said, "Don't."

"My husband," she said, "is stubborn as a mule. He likes fighting about everything."

He said, "No, I don't."

"See," she said, "he will fight about even that. Sit down, baby. He said you were thin as a rail. Let me fatten you up."

The meal was wonderful. Spicy and rich and the flavors were deep. And the wine flowed freely.

As we ate, she said to me, "You don't look happy, baby. What's wrong?"

"Well," I said, "I'm tired. Very tired."

I don't usually complain, but the good food and wine opened me up. Perhaps I didn't realize how tired I was. Tears came to my eyes. I said, "Each miracle takes something out of me. I'm exhausted."

She said, "Really? I thought you just waved your hand and..."

"One would think but no," I said. "I am learning you have to feel the other person's pain to understand it. You have to take it within you. Digest it. Reason with it. Reverse it. I don't know how many more miracles I can do."

She said, "You should stop now. They don't do any good anyway. No one has ever believed in anything because of a miracle."

I said, "What about parting the Red Sea?"

She said, "As soon as we were through and out the other side, we were complaining and saying, 'What have you done for me lately?'"

I asked Nathan, "Is your wife an expert on the scriptures?"

He said, "My wife is an expert on everything. It's my cross to bear."

She insisted, "Miracles will get you nowhere. They will change no one."

"What will?"

"*Meals*. Cooking. Get people together around a good meal and they will become friends for life. You should become a *cook*!"

I said, "Perhaps you're right. I once wanted to be a baker."

She said, "You should go back to that."

Nathan fell asleep at the table.

When Hannah had roused Nathan enough for him to go to bed, he said, surprised, "This? This has been a good night. I wasn't expecting this."

Afterward, Hannah and I sat and spoke quietly, intimately. She had a way about her: she was easy to talk with. She said, "What's on your mind, honey?"

I said, "I don't know if you'll understand. I don't want to be a cook. Or a baker. I want to be the meal."

I stopped, feeling foolish. She wasn't laughing. She was listening. So I went on.

"I want to be food. I want to be food for my people. I want to be bread. I want them to take what I am and nourish them, my people. Does that sound very odd?"

She said, "Not at all. I have had children. I have been their food. And my blood has pulsed through their veins. My children—other children as well—have sucked milk from my breasts. Every woman would understand what you feel."

"It's not foolish?" I asked.

"No," she said. "But it is inconvenient that you are a man."

We sat in quiet.

The quiet deepened until she said, "You felt my husband's pain?"

I nodded.

"Then you know," she said, "you know that I am his pain."

I nodded.

"And his joy," I said.

She shook her head no. "Maybe once."

"I wake up in the morning," she said, "and I wonder, 'Who can I love today?' Perhaps I loved too much. And, yes, sometimes I loved behind Nathan's back. But people need to be loved."

"You cheated on Nathan," I said.

She said, "I never cheated Nathan on love. I always loved him.... Still we have not slept in the same bed for a very long time. He was going to divorce me. Tonight, I thought. Now maybe it will be tomorrow."

I shook my head no. "Go to his bed tonight."

She said, "No. Not if he doesn't want me."

I said, "Go to his bed. While I was curing his dropsy, I took care of his other problems as well. I cured it all. Perhaps that's why I am so tired. And, yes, he was going to throw you out tonight. That's why I had to cure him on the sabbath."

She smiled. I smiled.

She said, "We're two of a kind, we are, you and I. We can never love enough."

Then she laughed. I asked why.

She said, "You can't read my thoughts?"

I shook my head no.

She said, "I was just looking at you and thinking, 'If I were thirty years younger...'"

I said, "Be good."

And we both laughed.

She invited me to stay the night and made me up a bed.

Then she went into her husband's bed—their bed—and slipped under the covers.

I left before dawn.

Before I left, I looked in on them and they were sleeping comfortably, arms tangled around each other.

I sat on a hillside waiting for the sun to rise, wondering, who will I love today?

Love, Death, and Agriculture

"Very truly, I tell you, unless a grain of wheat falls into the ground and dies, it remains just a single grain; but if it dies, it bears much fruit."

—John 12:24

I heard a woman in the front of the crowd say to someone, "I thought he was going to be talking about God but he seems to be going on about farming."

I went on about farming.

Another woman said, "It's because he's a man. Men can never say what they're thinking."

"Give him time. He'll get there," another woman added.

The first woman chimed in again, saying, "Well, I can tell you this. If I asked my husband where he was last night and he said to me, 'A seed is very small but, if you plant it, it grows into a tree and the birds can make their home in it,' I'd have him out the door before he could finish his story."

Another said, "It's what men are like."

I know when I am defeated. I stopped.

I said, "Ultimately, it's about love. Love one another."

The first woman said, "Did anybody get that from 'the seed falling in the ground'?"

They all shook their heads no.

A man said, "I've heard you preach. You never speak of love."

I said, "I do. I say love your enemy. Love others as you love yourself."

"Yes," he said, "but I have a wife, and I tell her I love her. And my children. I never hear you say, 'I love you.'"

A woman asked, "Have you ever been in love, prophet? Jeremiah, Isaiah, Ezekiel. None of them talk about their love. Woe this and woe that. And politics. Tell us about love."

"Well," I said, "The first time I fell in love, I began to injure myself at work. I accidentally took off the top of one of my fingers with a sharp chisel. My father was annoyed. He asked me what I had been thinking about and I didn't know. My mother said, 'He's in love.' I had to go away and think. I discovered that I was actually thinking about a young woman named Deborah."

They were more interested in this than the parable of the sower. Frankly, so was I.

"I went to Deborah with my bloody finger and said, 'Look what I did because of you.'"

One of the women said, "That's the least romantic story I have ever heard."

I shook my head. "She understood. She put two stitches in my finger and we spent the day together. She said she couldn't keep her mind on chores either and found herself feeding good food to the pigs. We were fascinated by each other. We spent days and nights learning one another."

One of the women ended the story for me. "And you married her?"

"No, I frightened her. She had opened me to love. But it was to a love that I felt not just for her but for every person I met. I told her that, and it frightened her. Me as well. It ended after that and left me lonely. But I would rather that I be lonely instead of her. If she had married me, she would have been very lonely."

A man who had been listening very carefully said, mysteriously, "I think I have heard the other half of this story. What was her name again?"

I said, "Deborah."

He asked, "Would you like to meet her again?" and invited me home to dinner to meet his wife, Deborah.

I went with some trepidation.

I did not recognize her immediately. She was, of course, the same and, at the same time, transformed.

Deborah said, "Welcome, Joshua. Sit. I'll have dinner ready shortly."

As she served dinner, I said, "I don't know what to say."

David said, "Anything but a parable! Tell my wife what you said today about her. It needs to be said."

I said to Deborah, "You opened an enormous space in me that I did not know was there. Even God—as I understood God—was small compared to the wonder of you. I told my rabbi this and he told me never to say it again. But I did. And those who understood became my friends. And the love, as it grew, became the love of God. And then the cures began..."

Deborah asked, "And you couldn't have had all that with me?"

I said, "I would have made a poor husband."

She said, "You might have let me decide that."

I said, "Forgive me. I was young." I asked, "Are you happy?"

Deborah nodded, "When my husband and children don't treat me as their maid. I torment my husband by telling him our oldest might not be his."

She smiled; David did not.

I asked, "Has love brought you happiness?"

She said, "It has brought me as much loneliness as joy. Passion can be exhausting.

"David told me your story about the seeds and how they grow. I have always understood you, Joshua. I think I understand your story. Let me tell you my version.

"My husband is a good man. He loves me. And I thought I knew what love was in loving him.

"When we had our first child, I realized how little love I had felt before.

"The same with the second child. And the third.

"And then the first child died.

"I could have used you then. I could have used a miracle.

"I had no idea how much love I could feel. How much love I needed. How vast the pain of love could be. And the joy."

We sat in silence.

I said to her husband, "Do you mind our having this conversation?"

He said, "No. I'm grateful. You did me a great favor once. Deborah wouldn't have looked at me if she hadn't been on the rebound from you. I think she married me to save face. But I love her, and she has come to love me. And as for this meeting? It's now ten years later. She has to stop thinking of you as this twenty-year-old boy. I suspect that you have to stop thinking of her as the one who is broken-hearted over you."

David said, "This needs to be over. You need to see each other as the simple people you are."

I said to David, "You've failed in that. I still think your wife is a miracle."

Deborah said, "I feel the same way toward you."

I said, "And now it is time for me to go."

David asked, "Is it over?"

I said, "It's over."

He asked, "Do you envy me?"

I said, "Absolutely. Do you envy me?"

He said, "Not at all. I see what is going to happen."

Then he asked with great sympathy, "Do you understand your own story?"

I nodded.

I didn't have to explain.

This should have been a moment of sadness, but what an enormous relief to know that they didn't think for a second that I was talking about agriculture.

Woman of the Parables 2

Then some people came, bringing to him a paralyzed man, carried by four of them. And when they could not bring him to Jesus because of the crowd, they removed the roof above him; and after having dug through it, they let down the mat on which the paralytic lay. When Jesus saw their faith, he said to the paralytic, "Son, your sins are forgiven."

—Mark 2:3–5

"It's all well and good for you, but what about the hole in my roof?"

She had a point.

Ever since I was little when she used to babysit me, Ruth always had a point. I thought Ruthie was a hundred years old then. God knows how old she is now. But since I was visiting home, I wanted to stop by and say hello.

I said, "It's not my fault they tore off your roof."

She said, "That's always what you used to say after the trouble you'd cause. Now you come here. I serve you tea. Then the next thing I know, you've got all your friends here. And their friends. And then you start preaching. And I have to serve them food."

I said, "You don't have to do that."

"Well, you're telling them to give everything away. How does that make me look if I don't serve them something? I'm exhausted from baking."

I said, "You have a generous heart and always did."

"You blackmailed me into it."

"You have a wicked tongue and a generous heart."

"But what about my roof?"

I told her I'd fix it. So I went home to get some tools that I hadn't used in some time. When I got back carrying the tools and a ladder, there was a young man waiting at the door. He was a working man, not the kind of person you would expect to drop to his knees—which is what he did— and kiss my feet and then my hands.

Ruth appeared at the door and said, "Treat him that way and he'll get a swelled head."

The young man said, "This man did a miracle. How can you say that?"

She said, "Well, he didn't do one for me, and I've known him since he was what? Well, since he *was*."

I said, "I can't do anything about old age."

She said, "And he insults me," and then went about her business.

I said, "Get up," and he did.

I said, "I'm Joshua." He said, "Yes, I know. We all know. I'm Reuben." He said, "There is so much in my heart that I would like to say to you."

I waited.

He couldn't speak.

"You can say what you like to me."

He said. "I can't."

I said, "You're one of the men who brought the boy to me."

He nodded and said, "I have never seen anything like what happened."

"Well," I said, "I've never seen faith rip a hole in a roof before."

He said, "I'm not sure if it was faith or desperation. Davey did *not* want to come. He was dead set against it. When he saw the crowd, he wanted us to go back home immediately. He was mortified up on the roof."

I looked up and said, "Speaking of which..." and put the ladder up against the house.

Reuben grabbed the tools from me. He said, "Don't be absurd. You? Repairing a roof? Impossible."

I said, "Well, I'm all out of miracles, the roof needs fixing or Ruth won't speak to me. And I'm a carpenter. But you can help if you'd like."

Actually, I was glad of the help. The ladder needed steadying and, when we started to work, I had trouble holding the hammer.

He said, "What's wrong?"

I said, "Cures? They take energy. You have to feel what the person is feeling."

"The pain?" he asked.

I said, "Yes, of course. But more than that, you feel the sheer raw animal hope. Davey might have been saying he didn't want to come, but everything in him was praying that I could be of help and dreading that I couldn't. I don't know how he contained so much feeling."

"Well," he said, "Davey has a very big heart."

As we worked, he asked, "Why did you say you'd forgive sins first?"

"Oh," I said, "I find people carry great burdens. Always dealing with misfortune, there is guilt; frequently shame.

That has to be addressed first. What happened to him? I can tell he wasn't this way from birth."

"How can you tell?"

"When children are born different, they adapt to whatever their issues are. Davey wasn't like that. His resilience was damaged as well as his body."

"Well, when he was young he was hurt in a climbing accident. It was his brother's fault actually. Davey always wanted to do what his big brother did, and his big brother is an idiot and didn't watch out for him well enough. It's possible the big brother was even showing off some to impress his friends, a girl maybe, by running along the edge of a cliff. And maybe he looked away when his brother tried to imitate him and fell."

I said, "His brother must bear a great burden."

He nodded and said, "I am his brother."

I said, "Yes. And when I said your sins are forgiven, I wasn't talking to Davey; I was talking to you."

He said, "I know ... I know."

As we worked, tea and cakes appeared through the hole in the roof.

I said, "I preach that all men are brothers but I'm an only child. I have no idea what I am talking about. Tell me about it. Tell me about having a brother."

"Well," he said, "you resent him at first. A younger one. I mean, he just appears. You didn't ask for him. Then you get used to him. You tolerate him. But after a time, you come to realize the beauty of the kid. You feel his dependence on you. You come to look at the child the way you would at a sunset. You didn't know your life was incomplete. You had thought you were complete. Now you know you were utterly empty. How would you live without him?"

He looked at me and said, "You asked what I was feeling. This is what I feel toward you, my brother."

I said, "I would be honored to be your brother if you would accept me."

"If as great a man as you would be willing to have as insignificant a man as me as your brother, then gladly."

When we fell silent, we heard a voice from below. "You're going to have to widen the door to get his head through it if you keep saying things like that to him."

We sat and looked at one another.

I reached for his hand.

I held it in both of mine.

He placed his other hand on mine and we sat.

I said, "Brother."

He said, "Brother."

As he left, Ruth gave him a package of food to take with him. "This is for your little brother. Don't eat it on the way. And this is for you to tide you over."

Leaving, he said to me, "How will I live without you, now that I know you are what I have been missing my whole life?"

I answered, "How did I live before I met you, not knowing what it was to have a brother?"

As he walked away, I said to Ruthie, "He's a good boy."

She said, "When he's not tearing holes in people's roofs."

I said, "You're a mean old woman."

She said, "And you are a badly-behaved child."

I left with the cake she baked me and her words in my ears, "Come back and build me a mansion someday!"

Beggar at the Gate

There was a rich man who was dressed in purple and
fine linen and who feasted sumptuously every day. And
at his gate lay a poor man named Lazarus, covered with
sores, who longed to satisfy his hunger with what fell from
the rich man's table; even the dogs would come and lick
his sores. The poor man died and was carried away by
the angels to be with Abraham. The rich man also died
and was buried. In Hades, where he was being tormented,
he looked up and saw Abraham far away with Lazarus
by his side. He called out, "Father Abraham, have mercy
on me, and send Lazarus to dip the tip of his finger in
water and cool my tongue; for I am in agony in these
flames." But Abraham said, "Child, remember that
during your lifetime you received your good things, and
Lazarus in like manner evil things; but now he is
comforted here, and you are in agony. Besides all this,
between you and us a great chasm has been fixed, so that
those who might want to pass from here to you cannot do
so, and no one can cross from there to us."

—Luke 16:19–26

Occasionally my mother would come to hear one of my sermons. She would stand at the back of the crowd with her arms crossed, looking skeptical.

It's hard to impress your mother.

Afterward I asked her what she thought about this one.

She said, "I wonder what you accomplished. Everyone knew who you were talking about. Hezekiah, the Pharisee and the beggar at his gate. I'm ashamed to say I don't know his name. Are you are trying to scare Hezekiah into caring for the beggar?"

I said I was.

"Do you think it will work?" she asked.

I said, "Yes. Don't you?"

She said, "Well, your father and I were never able to scare you into anything. I don't see why you'd think what didn't work for you would work for somebody else."

"What else can I do?" I said. "It's a scandal. I have confronted him personally. He says he has never seen a poor man at his gate. A lazy man? Yes. A man who doesn't want to work? Yes. Somebody has to say something harsh to him. So I took him on in public. I spoke strongly. I consider myself brave for having done it."

She said. "Invite Hezekiah for dinner."

I said, "Are you going to speak with him?"

She shook her head and said, "Tell him there's someone you want him to meet."

"Who?" I asked.

She looked at me as if I were simple.

She said, "The beggar at the gate."

Now this is the last thing I wanted to do, but she had turned her back and there is no arguing with my mother's back.

I brought the beggar, Marcus—a Roman as it turned out—to the house an hour earlier than Hezekiah, so she had time to clean him up, cut his hair, tend his wounds, put him in clothes of my father's so that when Hezekiah arrived, he didn't even recognize the man.

The food was predictably wonderful.

Dinner was amicable until Hezekiah asked Marcus what he did for a living.

I wanted to intervene but my mother gave the smallest shake of her head.

Marcus said, "I don't do much."

Hezekiah said, "You should. It's a good market. You could make a killing."

Marcus raised his eyes from his food and said, with an edge of judgment, "Like you?"

Hezekiah good-naturedly answered, "I am not ashamed to say it. When it comes to business, I have a killer instinct."

Marcus nodded.

There was silence.

I wanted to fill it.

My mother, though, waited. She waited deeply for Marcus to speak. And he did—simply, but from the depths.

Marcus said as he ate, "Killer instinct. I suppose that's my problem. I lack the instinct of a killer. But I have killed. Actually killed. But without the instinct, it's hard. I was a soldier once. I made good money. Killing pays well in Rome. But I didn't have the heart for it and eventually I gave up—not just on soldiering, but on everything. Everything ends in death, as the preacher said. So what's the point of doing anything? I sit quietly and try to be invisible. At least I was invisible until the preacher dragged me into the light."

Hezekiah asked, "How do you support your family?"

Marcus said with a smile, "I don't have one. It is the great sorrow of my life."

I was about to speak. My mother gave me the side eye.

Hezekiah said, "What a shame. My family is the joy of my life. I do everything I do for my family. I work night and day for my family."

Marcus spoke quietly.

He said simply, factually, eating all the while, "Your son sneaks out at night over the wall. At least, he used to. Now he doesn't even bother to sneak. He knows you aren't paying attention to him, so he just walks out at night and comes back in the morning. Your daughter receives callers at all hours. I know you give your wife expensive presents, but she sells them because she doesn't want rich things. She just wants to take care of the children."

Marcus kept eating. Hezekiah had stopped. Hezekiah said, "None of this is true. Why are you making this up?"

Marcus's silence was proof of the truth of what he had said. He had no need to defend or elaborate.

Hezekiah demanded, "Are you a spy? Is this a trap? Who are you?"

And I thought, "Oh, my God, you really never have seen him, have you?"

Marcus said, "I am the beggar at your gate."

And the Pharisee saw the beggar. Actually saw him. For the first time, he saw the man he had walked by every day for months.

My mother had the faintest smile.

"Who am I?" said Marcus quietly. "I am a man who envies you. Not your money. But your family. So I look after them. I sit at your gate and I counsel your son. He knows I was a soldier and he respects me. I talk to the young men who come to see your daughter. Her callers know I was a soldier and they heed me. When your wife can't sleep, we talk. It's what beggars do. They talk. They see. They visit."

Ashamed, Hezekiah said, reaching for his purse, "Well, I will certainly pay you for your services."

Marcus said, "My services are not for hire."

"Well, then, I will give you a job."

Marcus said, "I'm not in the market for a job. I do what I do because it pleases me to do it."

Hezekiah said, "Well, then, what do you want?"

Marcus said soberly, "I want this to be over. I want to be gone. I want to be done and go to the hell that God has specially prepared for people like me, for people who have done what I have done."

My mother did not have to look at me. I knew I did not have anything to speak to this. The words of life would have to come from Hezekiah.

After some thought, Hezekiah used his business persona to say, "Well, we cannot have that. We can't have you dying on my doorstep. I evidently need you to look after my family. I won't insult you by offering you money. But if you come to the back door, I will see you have food. You will be treated as part of the household. Which it seems you already are."

Marcus nodded.

Hezekiah rose. "I will go now, preacher. I am too ashamed to stay."

Marcus said, "Do not be too ashamed. Had you not been a bad father, I would have been very lonely."

Hezekiah said again, humbly, "Again, you shame me."

Marcus said, "I have been ashamed so long I know no other way to feel."

And they saw one another clearly.

And a great space opened.

But it did not divide them.

It embraced them.

The parting between them was awkward, as it must be when intimacy is both sudden and total.

Marcus remained and finished his meal.

My mother wanted him to keep my father's clothing. He said he couldn't. "Who would give money to a beggar in such beautiful clothing?" He folded my father's clothes and handed them back, with thanks, to my mother.

While cleaning up in silence, my mother said, mostly to herself, "I know a woman who works at that house. She is looking for a man. He may have a family yet."

I asked if there were anything else she wished to teach me, besides that a meal is a better teacher than a scolding.

She said, "In your story, once we die, a great gulf is fixed between the good and the bad. The unloved cannot be helped by those who loved."

I said, "Yes."

She said, "You're wrong, little one. Perhaps that was a story we told you to frighten you. That beggar—the one in your story—he would have found a way to get water to that man. He would have gotten around God in the long run."

I said, "You believe that life goes on beyond death?"

She said, "I believe that tenderness once begun never ends. I suppose there is no way of knowing until one dies, but I believe that. When I die, I will move heaven to see you fed, to keep you company."

I said, "And to correct my preaching?"

She said, "When needed."

That night, as we said good night, I promised her that, when I die, I would come looking for her. No matter what.

She said. "No need to look. I will always be there with your father, looking over your shoulder. No need to look for me. But look for him. Look for them. Look for the beggars at the gate."

The Miracle that Failed

He could not do any miracles there, except lay his
hands on a few sick people and heal them.

—Mark 6:5

Sorrow was usually enough. Sorrow drew something out of me, and she walked in great sorrow.

If I could cure her husband, I certainly would.

I stood and waited for the small procession to arrive.

They stopped in front of me.

But, to my surprise, this was not a sick man they were bringing to me. This was death, so I did what little I could. I prayed the Book of Wisdom from the depth of my soul:

The souls of the righteous are in the hand of God and no torment shall touch them. They seemed, in the view of the foolish, to be dead; and their passing away was thought an affliction and their going forth from us, utter destruction. But they are in peace.

As I opened my wet eyes, they met the woman's dry, unsatisfied eyes.

She said, "And is that all from the great wonder worker? A prayer? Said prettily? Any rabbi can do that. You are supposed to be something new."

I said, "I am not a rabbi. I am not even a teacher. I am the least of the least."

She said, "And you hide behind false modesty. You know you are something out of the ordinary. No one knows what to make of you. You are like a comet in the sky that no one can interpret."

I was forced to say, "No one less than I."

She said, "Well, this will tell us."

She pulled back the sheet and revealed the body.

I felt two things at once. The first—the absolute frightening presence of death. This was not a body. This was a cadaver. A dead thing beyond any hope.

The second, this was not her husband but her son. The son did not show any sign of illness. He had not wasted away. He died in his prime.

I asked, "Of what did he die?"

She did not speak. She rolled the blanket lower and revealed a sword wound below his ribs. A thrust there would have entered his heart and killed him quickly. He was killed by someone schooled in killing.

I asked, "A thief or a soldier?"

She said, "The latter."

I asked what she would have me do more than pray.

She said, "You can keep your prayer. I want my son back. You can have my life if it will help. I do not require him for long. I was there when he was born to welcome him. I wish to be there when he dies to kiss him farewell. Can you do this?"

I had cured. But this? Was it blasphemy even to attempt this? And, I admit, I was frightened of this corpse. Even so, I took the young man's hand. Has anything ever been colder? Or more stiff?

A crowd had gathered to watch by this point. I could feel their faith and their skepticism warring. Or perhaps that was happening only within me.

Holding the young man's hand, I closed my eyes. I closed them tight. I needed bravery for the effrontery I was about to perform. I was about to quote scripture to God. I reminded God that *the souls of the just are in the hands of God.*

I felt the size of what I was asking, but I also felt God's disturbance at the boy's death.

In the eyes of the foolish they seemed to have died . . .

Seem, I reminded God. *Seem. They only seem to have died . . .*

I felt warmth returning to the young man. No one was aware of this but me. I froze for a moment. Was his coldness moving into me? Frightened, I almost let go of the boy's hand, but the hand wouldn't let me. Then, perhaps a faint breath. Perhaps not. I could hear murmurs from the crowd, so, perhaps.

For though in the sight of men they were punished, their hope is full of immortality.

I felt God's desire to release this man from his own hands and back into the hands of his mother.

In the time of their visitation they will shine forth and will run like sparks through the stubble.

I could feel his grip, which had been faint like the grip of a child, strengthening into the grip of a man. He was pulling himself toward life and I was his anchor.

They will govern nations and rule over peoples, and the Lord will reign over them forever.

Then . . . Then, I felt the grip slipping.

I reached. He reached. But the grip faded.

Was this my lack of faith?

Or perhaps the young man's unwillingness to return?

Perhaps God's own helplessness before death.

But he had approached for a moment. I knew that. I could still feel his warmth.

Had it been enough?

I was too frightened to open my eyes.

Blind Bart

*They came to Jericho. As he and his disciples and a
large crowd were leaving Jericho, Bartimaeus son of
Timaeus, a blind beggar, was sitting by the roadside.
When he heard that it was Jesus of Nazareth, he began
to shout out and say, "Jesus, Son of David, have mercy
on me!" Many sternly ordered him to be quiet, but he
cried out even more loudly, "Son of David, have mercy
on me!"*

—Mark 10:46–48

If one more person asks me for a cure, I will scream.

The last half dozen times I have prayed for a miracle, I
have been denied. Ever since I realized it was possible for
me to fail, healing has become terrifying. I never know what
is going to happen. And that is not the only cause of terror.
I just told the disciples that I am going to be killed. I did not
get their sympathy. They are fighting over who will get to be
king of the kingdom. Madness. Failure on all sides. It is at
that point that I hear the cry, "Son of David, have pity on
me!"

I think if I just ignore whoever this is, he will go away.
I keep walking. No such luck. An insistent voice keeps
shouting, "Son of David, have pity on me!"

Walk.

"Son of David..."

The disciples, to their credit, have tried to quiet the voice.

"...have pity on me!"

It will not be quieted.

"Son of David, have pity on me!"

I have no pity, but I sigh and say, perhaps out of shame, "Bring him to me."

The crowd parts and I see that this thunderous sound has been coming out of a skinny, pitiable young man, far younger than I had expected and, as I say, skinny. And oppressed. And sad. With huge vocal power. Bass notes that could shake you to your bones. And enormous vacant eyes.

When I call for him, this young man does an odd thing. He hurls his cloak aside, leaps to his feet with huge energy and runs to me.

I don't know if you have ever seen a blind person run, but it's quite the show.

He stumbles. He tumbles. I am afraid he is going to hurt himself, but he doesn't care. He runs at me and, thinking it's me, grabs Peter tight around the waist. Peter pulls back and the blind boy spins around, now disoriented, and grabs a woman who shouts and backs away.

The young man desperately runs around the circle grabbing at arms, legs, torsos, whatever body part or piece of clothing he can catch hold of.

Before long, everyone is laughing like children at a game with a blindfolded contestant.

Everybody runs.

He runs after them.

All, including the blind boy, all are now laughing.

I don't run. I stand still.

Eventually, he finds my stillness.

His hands explore me.

I allow him to.

His hands explore my face.

I say, "Who are you? Everybody says your name is Blind Bartimaeus, son of Timaeus, as if 'Blind' were your first name and 'son-of-Timaeus' were your last."

He laughs and says, "I've been blind from birth, so that's the blind part. And my father is a builder, a wealthy man. He started out as a carpenter. Everybody knows Timaeus, so that's why they always call me his son. My friends call me Bart. Please call me Bart."

I ask why, if his father is rich, he makes his son beg.

An older man shouts, "He doesn't."

The young man explains, "Oh, he doesn't make me beg. I want to contribute something and the only thing I can do is beg. I tried to work as a child. I tried to use the tools in my father's shop. But I cut myself with the chisel and pounded my fingers with the hammer. See, I didn't know yet I was blind. I didn't know what "blind" meant." He showed me his hands. "These cuts and divots and scars are what taught me. So I beg. It isn't easy. People don't give money to a beggar whose father is the wealthiest man in town, no matter how pitiable I make myself look."

I ask what he wants from me, and his face shows he thinks I'm an idiot.

He says, "I want to see."

I am exhausted. I know I don't have a miracle in me. I explain that to him. I explain that I don't want to raise false hope in him.

He says, "But you don't *know* there is no miracle in you, do you? You are afraid of trying. You are afraid people will laugh. Why should that bother you? None of these people has even ever tried to do a miracle. Who knows what miracles lay within them undone for lack of trying? Why be afraid of their laughter?"

The crowd's laughter fades.

Their eyes are on me.

"Son of David?" he says, not loud now, quietly, just for me, "Son of David? Have pity on me."

His blind eyes face me for a moment. And then he lowers his head and waits.

What could I do?

I close my eyes and I pray inside to my father, "Father of David, have pity on me. Have pity on Bartimaeus. Have pity on us all."

I cry out. And I cry out. And cry out. I cry out until I cry.

But I get no answer.

Only laughter.

All I hear is laughter.

I wonder if people are openly laughing at me.

Has it come to that?

They have been discreet until this point.

But when I open my eyes, I see the laughter is not directed at me.

Bartimaeus is running, like a crazy person, from man to woman to man to woman trying to figure out who is who.

He can see.

And everyone is laughing.

And even I am laughing, though, as I now see, not everyone is.

A woman is crying because Bartimaeus is telling her how unimaginably beautiful she is. And she's crying because she's an old woman now and on the best day of her life she probably wasn't anyone's idea of beauty.

He insists.

Now everyone is weeping except Bartimaeus.

He stops in the middle of the circle that has formed around him. He looks at me, puzzled, and says, "They don't know, do they?"

I ask, "What?"

He says, "How beautiful they are."

And I say, "No. They don't."

And he asks, "You do?"

I nod and say, "Yes, I do."

Then, after a moment, he says, "Well, let's get going."

I ask him, "Where?"

And he says, "I'm going to follow you, of course."

I laugh. "What good would that do? One blind beggar following another. No, stay here."

"And do what," he asks. "Carpentry?"

I say, "If you like. It doesn't matter what. Be a carpenter. Be a beggar if you like. But keep looking at them. Seeing their beauty. And letting them see their beauty through you. That's what I have been trying to do for three years, but I haven't done it as well as you have in three minutes."

I look at him with my tired eyes.

And he looks at me with his fresh ones and I know what he is thinking.

And I wonder too what miracles wait undone within me.

The Death of an Angel

Immediately the king sent a soldier of the guard with
orders to bring John's head. He went and beheaded him
in the prison, brought his head on a platter, and gave it
to the girl. Then the girl gave it to her mother. When his
disciples heard about it, they came and took his body,
and laid it in a tomb.

—Mark 6:27–29

John was right—at least about himself.

Authorities would not allow him to go on.

They put him in prison.

Our prophet, the greatest prophet of the age, was, inevitably, going to be killed.

The question was: What should we do? Could we prevent it?

At which point, Peter had the worst of all his bad ideas.

He said, "Let's break him out!"

Like many of Peter's terrible ideas, there was an impulse behind it that was good and bold. So, after the disciples were asleep, I went to Joanna, one of the women who kept our whole enterprise afloat. Her husband, Chuza, managed Herod's household. To my surprise, she said that certainly she would help me.

"They are treating him like a wild animal," she said. "They are showing him off to everyone. 'This is our prophet. Come and see the prophet.' One more gawker won't make any difference. Tonight when they are drinking, I can get the keys. I can get you in."

I never asked Joanna where she obtained the money that supported us, but I got an idea of where it might have come from when I saw the palace. There was gold everywhere. Herod had built a monument to himself. Gold, gold, gold was on display everywhere. I assume some of it went walkabout and was supporting us.

Joanna let me into the dungeon and locked the door behind me.

When John saw me through the gloom, he smiled. Then he was horrified. "They've gotten you as well," he said.

I tried to reassure him. "No, cousin. I came to visit."

He tried to get me to leave immediately. I refused. I had a plan.

He said, "If you have come to get me to renounce my statements, I won't. You know I won't!"

I said, "Get you to renounce anything? When has that ever happened? I brought you some food."

John dismissed that. "They are all trying to fatten me up. They have nothing but food in this place."

I said, "I haven't brought you anything fattening. I brought you locusts and wild honey. Do they serve that here in your palace?"

He grabbed the bowl from my hands and began to eat hungrily. After a few mouthfuls, he stopped and held the bowl out to me apologetically. "Would you like some?"

I said, "You're the prophet. Not me."

As he ate, he asked the plan.

I said, "One of my disciples wanted us to stage a prison break."

John asked, "Could they do it?"

I said, "My disciples, if they tried, couldn't sink a leaky boat in a storm at sea."

He laughed for the first time and his warmth came through like a rising sun.

I said, "We can't stage a prison break. But we can get you out."

He stopped and asked with hope, "How?"

I said what I had been rehearsing all night. I said, "I will stay and you go."

I couldn't tell if John even understood me.

I repeated, "I will take your place tonight and, when they come in the morning, you will be gone."

Tears formed in his eyes. I had never seen John cry before.

I said, "I don't mean to make you sad."

He said, "I am not sad. I am crying because you would do that for me. And, knowing you, you would do it for anyone."

I said, "You're not just anyone, John."

He said, "I can't let you do it."

I said, "You can."

He said, "No. My life, all of it, has been to point to you and say—*him*. This is 'The One.' That is my job. It has been my job since before we were born. The first time we met we were still in our mothers' wombs. I leapt up when you came to visit."

I said, "You've been leaping your whole life. Are you sure it was me?"

He said, "Our mothers said so. And who would dare to tell them no?"

"But tell me," I asked, "If we are doing our jobs, why are you here? We both have been doing our song and dance as well as we can. I drank; you fasted. Yet here we are in a prison."

As he ate to the bottom of the bowl, he said, "Ah, well! That's authority for you. Herod as a ruler is a copy of his father. His father was a copy of his. With every copy, they get farther from justice. All God asks is that we become ourselves fearlessly, something that they are unwilling to do. God help us, we have become ourselves and that is always punished by those who haven't. But now, cousin, it's time for you to go."

Reluctantly, I nodded.

As I started away, he stopped me and said, "Before you go, one question."

I waited.

From his depths, he asked, "Are you 'The One,' cousin?"

Modesty would not do at this point.

It was a mark of his greatness that it was he who was imprisoned, not me, but this was not a moment to stand in his shadow; that would serve neither him nor me. So I stepped out of his shadow and told him the truth.

"The temple? It is no longer a building. It is here within me. The Ark of the Covenant? Within me. The tablets of the commandments, they are in me as well. The burning bush, the pillar of fire, all of them—within me. Adam and Eve? I feel their astonished love for one another and all the love since, licit and forbidden, real and imagined. I feel the hunger for justice of the prophets as well. All of it is within me."

As I spoke, I could see John's joy fill him. "Yes. That is it," he said.

"And yet I do not feel special. I feel that everyone can feel this if they let themselves become themselves as God is God. And, as you said, we desire, as God does, that they have life and that abundantly. . . .

"And you, John, you showed me this with your fasting and your honey. You split open a closed heaven and showed me God behind it. You held the sky open so that the spirit could descend and, when it did, you didn't grab for it. You let it fall into me. You opened heaven for me and God has claimed me.

"Like you, I am the wedge that will spilt the rock of the world as Moses struck the rock and water poured out. But I am also myself. I am the pelican who will feed its young with its heart's blood. I am a mother who will feed the world with her milk."

John said, "I would have said I am sorry not to have lived to have seen the promise fulfilled, but I have seen it now. And now you must go."

I said, "This is the last time I will see you."

He nodded.

I said, "Then goodbye, my cousin, my brother, my heart, my soul, my guide, my prophet, my priest, my friend."

John said, "And you, my little cousin, my lord, my God."

As I walked for the door, he shouted big-brotherly advice after me.

"Stay by the lepers! They can see what's wrong with an outsider's clarity. Stay with the poor! They can tell you what's wrong with the distribution of wealth. Stay by the widows. They will teach you about the callousness of men. Stay with the old. Trust their wisdom. But do not try to be another John the Baptist. One of them is plenty. Be only what you are. What you are is God."

I stopped at the door and said, "As are they all."

And he said, "As are they all."

And then...

"Thanks for the locusts and honey. It was a feast."

From the days of John the Baptist until now the kingdom of heaven has suffered violence and the violent take it by force.

—Matthew 11:12

I have preached badly today.

I didn't have the heart for it, but I preached anyway. Shame on me for speaking when there was nothing to say.

I was tired.

I was afraid.

I was enraged.

Contradictory emotions silenced me.

You see, they killed my friend.

My cousin.

My hero.

The one who baptized me.

We had known one another from before we were born.

Now he was gone.

They came and took him away.

Put him in jail.

On a whim, they cut his head off.

I wanted to shout revenge.

Revenge.

Revenge.

Revenge.

John would have shouted for vengeance.

I can't.

I don't understand that kind of a god.

He did.

So I talked nonsense about love.

Even I was bored with myself.

No one will remember what I said today.

No one will write it down.

So now I sit, as I did once before, with his head in my lap.

Joanna, the bravest disciple, smuggled it out of the palace.

And I sit and think about angels and what John once told me.

That I was an angel.

You were wrong, John.

I am not an angel.

Angels don't die.

Labor Pains

*When a woman is in labor, she is in anguish because
her hour has arrived, but when she has given birth to a
child, she no longer remembers the pain because of her
joy that a child has been born into the world.*

—John 16:21

So great is the joy of having a child that a woman forgets the
pains of the birth.

I had said this many times while preaching, but one day,
the minute I said a woman forgets her labor pains, a hand
shot up and a woman shouted, "Wait a minute."

All eyes went to her.

Peter said, "He'll take questions after."

But I said, "Go on."

The woman—whom I had never seen before but looked
familiar—said, "I have a question. Are you *sure* women don't
remember labor pains? I mean have you ever spoken with
your mother about that?"

I said, "I'd find that awkward to bring up, but she seems
very glad I'm here and she's never brought up the pain."

The woman asked, "Does that mean she has forgotten?"

I said I didn't know.

"I was in labor for a night and a day," she said. "Yes, I

was joyous when the baby was born. But I certainly remember the pain. Very clearly."

And I said, "But you love your child."

And she said, "Oh, yes. I love my son. But he doesn't come to visit and treats me like I don't even exist."

"What a terrible son," I said.

At which point, James the Lesser, one of my disciples, said, "Leave it alone."

I said, "What?"

He said, "Leave it alone."

I said "Why?"

He said, "That's my mother."

I said, "I beg your pardon."

James said, "She's my mother."

And I said, "And you don't visit her? James? I'm disappointed in you."

James said, "Well, you said, 'Leave everything. Leave your father and mother. Whoever doesn't hate his father and mother and come follow me won't have eternal life.'"

And James's mother said, "Did he really say that?"

I said, "You have to consider the context—"

The disciples said, "Oh yes, he said that."

This was not going the way I had hoped.

James's mother, Irene (and I know now why she looked familiar—James was the image of her) said, "You know, you really shouldn't speak for women if you haven't asked them. If you're too embarrassed to ask your mother, I can tell you about my James's birth."

James the Lesser said, "Please don't."

But she did.

She said, "I almost died. It's not something I say often. None of us do. We risk our lives to have children. Many of us do die. Worse—many children die and we go on living.

When I thought I was going to die, my only concern was that the baby live. When I look back I can't believe how generous I was. That's what I remember. Now, James, here are your mended clothes and some spending money. Come home when you get a chance or when this man lets you. And you," she said to me, "you're welcome for a meal whenever you wish."

Then Irene gave James a kiss and off she went, leaving all of us sons feeling ungenerous and ungrateful.

I asked my mother about my birth—if it was a difficult birth.

She said, "For who?"

I said, "What do you mean for who? Was it a difficult birth?"

She said, "You seemed to think so. You made quite a lot of noise."

This was not going as I had planned either.

She said, "You father was very helpful."

"Really," I said. "He said he fell apart."

She said, "That was very helpful. He carried all the worry and anxiety for me so I could concentrate on having the baby. It was very hard work. Then, when it was over, you were very loud. The loudest child I have ever heard. I thought, 'Who is this child? This demanding, wild child?' But you calmed down at your first feeding."

She smiled at my father who was standing in the doorway. He smiled back.

She said, "I will never forget that. You were as happy at that moment as you were miserable a moment before. You were the picture of bliss. Your father and I laughed. You brought the two of us together deeply. And we knew what our lives would be. It was clear you were going to be a handful."

"So you forgot the pain," I said.

"I didn't forget the pain. I think I might have hallucinated to get past it. I saw angels and kings."

My father said, "I also saw them, so it must have happened —unless I was hallucinating too. We were very tired. Oh, son, how you cried."

My mother looked at me and said, "Babies are remarkably selfish. They think of nothing but themselves. Some grow out of that. Some do not. There were times I thought you would never grow out of it."

"Have I?" I asked.

She said, "I think you've gone too far in the other direction. There's no middle ground with you. Never has been."

My father said, "I wonder where he got that from?" and left the room.

And we sat together for a while.

She said, "When you go through it—birth—a part of you is born as well. A love you didn't know you were capable of. Of course, a part of you dies, but the love that is born is worth it."

I said, "Thank you."

"You're welcome," she said.

Then she said, "I hope any pain you will ever feel will be very much worth the effort."

I asked, "Did you know at the time it would be worth the effort?"

She shook her head and said, "You never know at the time."

I went to visit James the Lesser's mother a few years later.

By then I had gone through a great deal of pain and I hadn't known at the time if it would be worth the effort. Truly, I didn't.

But when it was all over, I felt I understood things more clearly. More simply.

I felt I owed Irene a visit.

I didn't knock.

I didn't even use the door.

I just appeared at her table.

She seemed to take it for granted that I was there.

She said, "Have you finally come for that meal?"

I said, "Forgive the delay."

As she prepared the meal, she snuck glances at my hands, my feet, my side.

Finally, I just showed them to her.

As she put ointment on them, she asked, "Do you remember the pain?"

I said, "It was a night and a day—how could I not remember?"

She asked, "Was it worth the effort?"

"Yes," I said. "I think it was. Of course, a part of you dies, but a love greater than you could imagine is born."

She nodded.

And we shared a meal.

The Groom Dances Alone

The disciples of John and of the Pharisees were
accustomed to fast. People came to Jesus and objected,
"Why do the disciples of John and the disciples of the
Pharisees fast, but your disciples do not fast?" Jesus
answered them, "Can the wedding guests fast while the
bridegroom is with them?"

—Mark 2:18–20

My goal was to unite people, but not like this. The followers of John the Baptist and the Pharisees hate one another, but they have come together in a common cause. Denouncing me. This was not the plan. They arrived together buzzing like hornets. They wanted to know why, since they fasted, I let my disciples eat and drink. So I told them. "It's all like a wedding."

They asked, "What is?"

I said, "The kingdom of God. It's a wedding feast."

They asked, "Have you been drinking?"

I said, "As a matter of fact, I have." I offered them the wineskin. They declined. I said, "Please drink. It's a wedding. God wishes to marry us all. To one another. God is in love with us."

They said, "Wedding? There is nothing in scripture about the kingdom being a wedding."

I said, "Well, perhaps there should be."

They said, "Besides, what would you know about a wedding? You've never been married."

I said, "True. I've been engaged twice, but never went through with it. You're all married. So teach me. Tell me what it's like to be a bridegroom."

They were quiet. Then one said with the bitterness of experience, "A marriage is nothing but trouble."

I said, "Perhaps. But a wedding? Tell me about your weddings."

Jonas, a middle-aged follower of my cousin John, broke the ice. He said, "Well, I, for one, I was terrified. And ashamed. I had no idea what to do that night. I was dreading it and desiring it equally."

Malachi, a devoted Pharisee, said, "Me? I knew exactly what to do. And I was a bit ashamed of myself for knowing."

Abimelech laughed and said, "I was very young. I didn't know enough to be frightened or ashamed. I simply couldn't wait to be alone with her—and not just for sex. I don't think I had ever had a private moment with her before that night. I was just glad to be rid of her mother and father and all those brothers. I didn't know if we would have anything to say to one another. But, you know what?" he continued. "Then I saw her. And then all these things went away."

All those husbands nodded in agreement.

The same, one said. The same, said another. Bliss, said one. Joy. Heaven.

I asked, "Did you eat at the wedding? Did you drink?"

They all said yes. "To excess."

"Why?" I asked.

Malachi said, "In my right mind, I couldn't be as happy as I wished to be. I wanted to let go of everything."

I asked, "Let go of what?"

They all answered differently.

Families did not get along. We were poor. We couldn't pay for the food. Abimelech said, "I was afraid that I wouldn't be worthy of her. But we ate and drank. And drank and danced. It was a wonder."

I asked, "Why can't it be like that? Why can't we see God as our greatest and deepest joy?"

And they responded with passion.

"Scripture!"

I said, "Instruct me."

They said, "You know! God is a refiner's fire. God is a pillar of fire. A mighty warrior. Saul slew his thousands; David his ten thousands. God freed us from bondage in Egypt. Praised be God who killed Pharaoh's first-born son and the first-born of all Egypt."

I said, "And you ask me why I drink?"

And I drank.

They said, "But this is scripture."

I said, "Well, then, scripture is wrong. We should tear it up. Or at least that part of it. My god is not a killer of children. My God said to Abraham, "Don't kill the child." That is scripture. Let Moloch kill. Let Baal. But not the God of Abraham. And anyone who says our God is a killer of children, even Pharaoh's children, blasphemes."

They turned from joy to rage, "You are the blasphemer! And you know what happens to those who blaspheme. Take it back!"

I said, "I have said what I have said."

And they left me.

Only one remained.

A rich, very rich, older man. He stayed. He said, "You know they'll be coming for you, don't you? Call them back. Repent."

I sighed, "I can't. I tried the other way. I went to Qumran. I was as pure as could be. I fasted. I washed five times a day. I wore bleached cloth until my skin was raw. I couldn't find God there. It's loose clothes and good companions for me."

He said, "Give me that wineskin," and he drank. He handed me back the skin and said, "I was at your parents' wedding."

I asked, "How was that?"

He said slyly, "You should know. You were there."

I asked, "Are you trying to shame me with my birth?"

He laughed. "Never. There was no shame that day. Or that night. Oh, people brought stones with them. In their pockets. Behind their backs. The pregnant girl. The man who was willing to protect her sin. But then they saw your father and mother."

I said, "Tell me about it. Tell me about my father."

He laughed.

"The men said, 'Look at that old man. If he can get such a beauty for a bride, there is hope for us all.'"

I said, "More. Tell me more. Tell me about my mother."

He said, "Give me the wine.... The women? They were prepared to scoff. But they saw your mother's joy. And they said, 'You know, the child's not his. He must love her very much. I wish I had a husband like that.'"

I asked, "Was she ashamed?"

He said, "Shame was banished.

"Enemies were forgetful of their hate. Businessmen forgot their competition. Yes, we all ate and drank together."

I said, "And my father danced with the men and my mother with the women, but they never took their eyes from one another."

He asked, "How can you know that? You weren't born yet."

I said, "No, but that's how they looked at one another every day until my mother returned my father to the earth. Pass the wine."

He passed the wine and said, "Yes, they danced that night. And when they went off together, all the men and all the women wanted to sleep with one another. It was the sexiest wedding I have ever attended. And the next morning people woke unexpectedly in one another's arms—and yet there was no shame."

I said, "Can we not be that way always? Can I not always be the bridegroom? The cause of such joy?"

He said, "You are very much your parents' child. You have the same beauty. The same joy. But I warn you, if you put new wine into old wine skins, the skins will burst. Those men? They are old skins and you are very new wine."

I said with a shrug, "I must be the groom. Until, at my wedding, all sit down at the same table. The sons of Pharaoh with the daughters of Sarah. Do you believe it can happen?"

He said, "Anyone will eat if the food is good enough and the wine potent. But, little one, I must ask you ... Why no wife? Aren't you lonely without a wife?"

I asked, "Aren't you lonely sometimes with one?"

He laughed and said yes.

I said, more bitterly than I intended, "I'll tell you why I never married any of the women I have loved. I have cared for them too much to make them early widows."

We were silent. Then I asked a favor.

He said, "Anything, little one."

I said, "When I die, there will be no wife or children to bury me. You are a man of means. Will you bury me?"

He laughed.

I asked, "Why are you laughing?"

He said, "I thought you were going to ask me to sell what I have and give to the poor."

I said, "I'm not that drunk."

He said, "Certainly I will see to your burial. And then I will drink in your honor. And dance."

I said, "No, you won't."

He said, "You're right. I will mourn the bridegroom. The beautiful groom."

I said, "You will be the only one. I will die young and be forgotten."

He said thoughtfully, "I think not. I think you will be remembered. And not just by me."

I said, "That consoles me."

He left.

And, alone in the street, I danced.

I shouted, "Come dance. Come dance with me. It is my wedding day."

And a few fools joined me.

The Exorcist

*Jesus left that place and went away to the district of Tyre
and Sidon. Just then a Canaanite woman from that
region came out and started shouting, "Have mercy on
me, Lord, Son of David; my daughter is tormented by a
demon." But he did not answer her at all. And his
disciples came and urged him, saying, "Send her away,
for she keeps shouting after us." He answered, "I was
sent only to the lost sheep of the house of Israel." But she
came and knelt before him, saying, "Lord, help me." He
answered, "It is not fair to take the children's food and
throw it to the dogs."*

—Matthew 15:21–26

She bit me! The little girl bit me!

As I checked my hand to see if she had drawn blood, the
mother laughed. I said, "Yes, yes, I should have known better. You told me your daughter was possessed. Still," I said
resentfully, "I have dealt with many possessed and I have
never been bitten."

The mother answered, "My daughter can be very sweet,
but it is her peculiar ailment that she will become whatever
you call her. Call her a stone and she will become silent. Call
her a slut and she will show herself to you. Call her a dog

and she will bite. You shouldn't have called her a dog, holy man."

I was about to say that I had not called her a dog, but I caught myself. The truth was I had. It had been automatic. Unthinking. Reflex. I excused myself, explaining that I was exhausted from this trip to Tyre, which was the farthest I had ever traveled from home. How else to explain why I would have responded when the mother asked me for help, "I have to look after the children of the house of David. It's not for me to give the children's bread to the dogs under the table." It's not like me to say such a thing.

The mother went on. "Maybe we are dogs. But even dogs eat, are petted, are cared for. Be as good to us as you would be to a dog and I will not ask for better."

Clearly there were apologies to be made.

I said to the daughter, "Your mother says you're a sweet girl." She responded sweetly with a small smile.

I asked her name. A woman from the watching crowd snickered, "Name? She probably doesn't even know that she has one. Or what one is." Her mother paid no attention. She coached her daughter. "Prove that fool wrong. Tell the holy man your name."

She wouldn't.

I said to the child, "Well, I have a name. Would you like to know it?"

She nodded her head.

"Come closer then and I will tell you."

I spoke quietly so she would approach. As she did, I said softly, "My name..." I held out my hand to her—the one she hadn't bitten—and said, "My name is Joshua."

And, quick as a flash, she bit my other hand and ran back to her mother who laughed louder.

The mother laughed on. "Bad start, holy man. Bad start, son of David."

I said, "What? Why this time? I was trying to do you good." Looking at the indentations on both hands, I asked, "What just happened?"

She said, "You don't want to know."

But I did.

"Fine, then," she said, "Do you know what your name Joshua means?"

I said with pride, "Yes, it means God's salvation."

She said, "Not to us. Do you know who Joshua of Jericho is?"

"Of course."

"Then tell me," she said.

I was annoyed to be given a test on the scriptures in the street by this woman.

"Joshua's the hero of the scriptures who blew his trumpet and the walls of Jericho fell."

She replied with ancient but potent anger, "Well, he wouldn't be a hero if you were living in that city when Joshua blew that trumpet and the walls fell down on them. On us."

Blinding light.

Suddenly, it all made sense.

I said, "You are a Canaanite."

She nodded.

I said, "But you can't be."

"I know," she said. "You thought you killed us all. But we are a hard people to kill."

I justified myself by saying, "That was a very long time ago. I did not do that." I turned to her daughter and repeated, "I didn't do that."

That seemed to reassure the girl, not the mother, who was not about to let me off the hook.

"Well, your God." She said, "Your God did that. You can't deny it."

What could I say?

Our God, the God I worship, had commanded Joshua to cross the Jordan and kill all the inhabitants of Jericho—men, women, children, even the dogs. Joshua did as he was commanded. We celebrate the moment in song.

And now in a flash as sudden as a bite, I knew why I had called her a dog.

I should have known the moment the word escaped my lips.

You are cruel to those you have wronged.

The mother spoke, "Your God proved his point. He was stronger than our god. But once that's done, what? You are right, it was a long time ago. It involved neither you nor me. But where does that leave us? What good is a powerful god if he cannot help one young girl?"

I felt the depth of the history separating me and this child. More humbly, I started over, realizing the immensity of the chasm that would have to be bridged between us. I did not know if it could be done.

I said to the girl, "I'm not that Joshua. Promise."

She nodded.

"You recognize—I won't say it again—my name." She nodded. "Then you *do* know what names are." She nodded. "I won't ask you to tell me your name since you don't want to, but maybe...maybe I can guess it."

She was sure I couldn't.

I began to guess names. Girls' names. No? More girls' names. No? Boys' names. She laughed.

She had no intention of telling me her name, but I insisted, "No, no, no. Don't tell me. No matter what. I will guess your name."

She came to me and sat in my lap.

Her mother said, "She likes games."

The disciples brought food and drink for me, the mother, and the girl.

I guessed names for hours.

She shook her head at every one.

She fell asleep in my arms.

The mother fell asleep on my shoulder. Before she did, she whispered to me the child's name, Rahab. The name of the Jericho prostitute who betrayed her people. Perhaps our victory wasn't because our God was stronger. Actually, I should have guessed Rahab first. I was glad I didn't.

Her mother said, "Rahab is her name. She knows it."

As they slept, I prayed through the night.

I found I was afraid.

Not of her.

Of my own word.

How did that word come to my lips?

My lips?

My lips that have proclaimed God's love, that have pronounced "Love your enemies," that have berated the disciples for not understanding that love is the beginning and end of all things. How could these lips have called her that name? A dog? If such a word can, unbidden and undesired, come out of me, one purified, anointed, proclaimed, is there any exorcist in the world capable of taking the history of hate out of a human heart?

The girl woke before her mother. I whispered confidently in her ear, "Rahab."

She surprised me by shaking her head no.

I thought for a moment that she might actually not know her name. But then she said quietly, so as not to wake up her mother.

"That's what *she* calls me."

I asked, "But that's not your name?"

She shook her head.

"Will you tell me?"

She said, "I won't tell anyone."

I asked, "But you know it?"

She nodded.

She said, "It's a beautiful name." Then she asked, "Do you have a secret name?"

I told her I did, in fact. Emmanuel—God with us. It was very secret and most beautiful, though perhaps not as beautiful as hers. I told her that I try to act in accord with my true name.

She said, "Guard it. Or they will take it from you."

I said, "But these are our secret names. Because we have them, we don't have to be what people call us, do we?"

She thought. And then she nodded in agreement.

I don't know what her hidden name was but, when her mother awoke, the mother found her daughter waiting for her calmly, cheerfully, even—if this can be said of a child— wisely.

The mother thanked me.

By the time we parted, the exorcism was successful.

The child had driven the demon out of me completely.

The Other Nine

Then Jesus asked, "Were not ten made clean? But the other nine, where are they?"

—Luke 17:17

"Where are the other nine?"

Why did I ask that? Where did that come from? I am turning into my mother. "Is this the thanks that I get?" How needy have I become?

In my defense, I could feel the catastrophe of my life beginning to collapse on me. I had been trying to explain this to the disciples, but when I talked about the end, they would drink themselves into a stupor. So from somewhere deep inside came the resentful tone and words, "Where are the other nine lepers?" I should just have said, "You're welcome" and moved on, which is what I then did.

But the leper threw my rhetorical question back at me.

She said, "Where are the other nine? I can tell you. Or you can tell me yourself because you very well know."

I tried and failed to keep resentment out of my voice. "I don't where they are or I wouldn't have asked."

She said, "Fine, then. You want me to tell you they were ungrateful and that's why they aren't here? A nice pat moral lesson? I could do that. Or I could tell you the real reason they're not here."

I asked, "Were you this argumentative as a leper?"

She said, "Always. I was not a popular leper."

Her honesty forced me to admit it. "Yes, I know why they didn't come back. The better question is: Why did you?"

She smiled. "That's easy. You told us to present ourselves to the priests. I didn't go to the priests. So I didn't have to hear them say, if you go back to the healer, you will be as marked for death as he is."

I said, "And why would they say that?"

"Because you healed ten lepers. Ten! Healing one leper, that's a kindness. Healing two, an act of great generosity. But healing ten? That's a *stunt*. That's a circus act. That's a *statement*. You're declaring war on them. Telling them that you are an irresistible power and that you are coming for them. And you are, aren't you? You are going to Jerusalem."

I asked, "Are the priests debating killing me?"

She said, "That was settled long ago. Now they are discussing how. They will be waiting for you in Jerusalem and they will fall on you like a hailstorm. That's why there were ten lepers seeking you. Every sick person in Israel will be looking for you now. Your time is running out. Everybody knows."

I asked, "If you didn't go to the priest, to whom did you go?"

She said, "You know that too."

I said, "You went and found yourself a man."

She laughed and said, "I did. Young and handsome. And it was far better than going to a priest on this occasion."

I said, "You didn't give thanks to God."

She said, "Perhaps that was my way. . . . I'll tell you why I came back."

Anxious to be gone, I said, "You have come back to thank me. No need to explain. Goodbye. Your faith has saved you."

She held her ground.

She said, "Why do you say that? 'Your faith has saved you.' You know it isn't true."

I was getting annoyed now.

"I have never met a person this anxious to dispute a miracle. I am starting to feel sorry that you came back. Go away."

She stood her ground.

She said, "It can't be my faith. If it had been, I would have been cured long ago. It was your faith that saved me."

"My faith?" Her honesty provoked mine. I confided in her. "I will tell you something I don't tell everyone. I have less faith every day. At the start I was full of faith. Now I have none. Or little."

She laughed and said, "Did you think I was talking about faith in God?"

She shook her head. "No. That's too easy. Me. Faith in me. You believed in me. You believed there was more to me than my disease."

I said, "Well, I'm grateful that you came back to thank me."

"I didn't," she said. "I will tell you why I came back."

I said, "At this point, I don't want to know."

She said, "Well, I'll tell you anyway. I want to learn how to do what you did. I will need a trade now. If I could cure, I could make a good living. I wouldn't charge exorbitantly. Just enough to keep body and soul together. How do you do it? How do you heal? What's the trick?"

She deserved an honest answer. Perhaps she could heal as well. She should know the difficulties.

I said, "It isn't one size fits all. Each case is different because, in each case, the pain is different. You have to, for a moment, live in the flesh of the other person. Let her blood flow through you. Everyone's pain is unique. Even all the lepers were different. You, for instance. I felt, not your sickness, but your agony. Your real agony. When you discovered your leprosy, you were thirteen. You left home to spare your family pain. You were too young for so great an act of generosity. It was a sacrifice greater than you were capable of. It left your heart broken. I healed that first. That was more demanding than the disease."

She asked, "And what is the healing?"

"I know how it starts. Then it is out of my hands."

"How does it start?"

I said, "It is life's desire to go on. The desire for life abundantly. It fills me and overflows."

She said, "I would call that sex."

I said, "Sex. Spirit. All those words that ultimately mean the same thing. But I am full of that desire. Life abundantly overflows my limits. Are you capable of that?"

She said, "Of course. What does a leper have but desire? And that healing? It's a two-way street. You didn't know that, did you?"

I said, "What do you mean?"

She said, "I also felt what was going on inside you. You are terrified of death. Not any death. *Your* death."

I thought I wanted a frank conversation about my death. Now I knew I didn't.

"Yes," I said, "I am afraid death is coming."

"Well," she said with a shrug, "there's no cure for death."

I said, "I'm hoping that isn't true."

She said, "I might be able to help you. You see, I know death. We lepers do. We have lived death. I know what it is to carry death in my body. Every person carries it. Most people deny that. You can't. That's why you are unafraid of us. And why we are unafraid of you. And why the priests are so desperately afraid of you."

I said, "And how can you help me?"

She said, "Kneel, healer. Let us switch places. Let me try your tricks on you."

I knelt before her. She ran her fingers through my hair. She whispered in my ear, "Yes, there is death. But you, you beautiful man, you are more than your death. So much more! You are so much more than your death that death fades into insignificance.

"But death's not the real problem, is it? Not the real agony. You're afraid that the priests are right after all, that you deserve your death. That you have lost your faith in God. And I am here to tell you, even if you lost your faith in him, believe in me. Look at me and know what you have done. The life in you has overflowed into me. Let me be the proof that you are right and they are wrong, no matter the cost. Believe in me. Me. I am here and I am undeniable, no matter what they might say."

Our eyes met.

Her love for me, her respect for me, the gratitude she offered me, in spite of her words, were all infinite.

Then she removed her hands, stepped back and asked, "How did I do?"

I took time. I looked within myself for fear. I looked within myself for regret. I looked within myself for death.

I said, "Now I know why you came back."

"Yes," she said. "I felt I had to return the favor. Fair's fair."

I said, "I thank you."

As she was leaving, she said over her shoulder, "No need. Now we are even, beautiful man."

I shouted after her, "Be good, sister. Be good."

She laughed and said, "Unlikely."

Her final words were spoken in laughter.

"Don't be afraid of death, beautiful man. Have pity on it. Death is afraid of you. Death is afraid it will die."

Why I laughed I do not know.

Woman of the Parables 3

*He sat down opposite the treasury, and watched the
crowd putting money into the treasury. Many rich
people put in large sums. A poor widow came and put
in two small copper coins, which are worth a penny.
Then he called his disciples and said to them, "Truly I
tell you, this poor widow has put in more than all those
who are contributing to the treasury. For all of them
have contributed out of their abundance; but she out of
her poverty has put in everything she had, all she had
to live on."*

—Mark 12:41–44

The disciples had been coming up to me saying, "For God's
sake, would you stop talking about dying. You are depress-
ing us. And please stop telling your followers that *they* are
going to die. It's a bad recruitment tool."

They thought I was in one of my moods, but they don't
understand. I separated myself from them. I needed someone to understand.

Then I heard laughter. A woman's laughter. I glanced toward her and almost missed her. She looked like a pile of
rags that had blown off a rag seller's cart. Almost invisible.
And she was delighted, laughing at me.

She said, "He-he! You're scared! Well, you should be! He's trying to see you, Herod. His father tried to kill you last time, and now the son is going to finish the job. He-he!"

I said, "Who are you? The devil?"

She said, "I used to be a friend of your mother. She told me how they had to run away in the night with you to protect you from Herod, the father. Now the son is looking for you and he gets what he wants. You're scared."

I recognized her through the dirt and the smell. She had been a poor but generous woman. Perhaps maddened by her own generosity. She couldn't help giving away what she had, and now she had nothing. And she was laughing at me.

I said, "Yes, I am scared. Why shouldn't I be? He killed my best friend."

"Simple enough, then," she said. "Run. Hide."

I said, "Not before I have done my work."

"What's that?"

"I want to protect the powerless."

"Protect us? Most people don't even see us. Well, I will give you credit. You, at least, notice. And you haven't moved away from my smell. People say we don't notice our smell because we have to live with it, but they're wrong. Help me clean up, Mary's son, and I will help you."

"Help me with what?"

"Your fear."

So I picked her up—she weighed nothing—and took her to a stream. I took off her rags. A woman by the stream took them and offered to wash them as best she could.

As I lowered her into the water, she said, "Oh, that feels good."

I asked, "How can you help me?"

She said, "You say you wish to take care of us? Elijah

didn't, outside of one lucky widow. Elijah did miracles. What did Elijah's miracles do? Or John's protests and prophecy? Great men make their own legacies, but they don't change ours. They became great. But they don't affect what happens to the powerless. You are becoming great, Mary's son. Will you forget us?"

"What can I do?"

As I washed her, an old shrewdness came into her eyes.

"We have committed no crime, but when we die, we are treated like criminals. We are thrown into the pit. Lime is tossed on our bodies. No chariot of fire for us. No one mourns for us, like your cousin John. But you? You? People would remember you. People would say about the men who did that to you...they would say such men must be held to account."

She waited for my response.

"Are you...are you asking me to die?"

"Pshhhh. Everyone dies," she said. "I am asking you to die with us."

"People have asked me to dinner with them, to weddings with them, to debate with them. No one has asked me to die with them."

"The poor have little else to offer. But if you are willing to die with us, you will have followers. And they will say, 'Here was an innocent killed for nothing.' You would interrupt the constant repetition of history. Prophets and kings shouting at one another throughout all time. People would take note."

"How will this make me less afraid?"

"It won't. But it would give meaning to your fear. You would not fear for yourself. You would be afraid for us. And we would love you for it. Be voiceless with us. Be one of us. Hold us as we hold one another. You would achieve what

John and Elijah did not with all their preaching and miracles. You would make us visible."

She was even less visible now that she was clean. Her skin was so thin that you could almost see light through her. Her dress was washed but wet, so the women wrapped her in clean white cloths before they went home to their families.

When we were alone, she died.

She breathed her last and died.

She had finally given away everything.

And no one noticed.

No one mourned.

There was no kind word.

There was only silence.

And I thought, "Who would have the courage to actually choose a death like this?"

Transfiguring

Six days later, Jesus took with him Peter and James and
John, and led them up a high mountain apart, by
themselves. And he was transfigured before them, and
his clothes became dazzling white, such as no one on
earth could bleach them. And there appeared to them
Elijah with Moses, who were talking with Jesus.

—Mark 9:2–4

When I awoke, I was in John's arms and he was calling my
name.

He held me so tight I couldn't breathe.

Peter was in the background shouting that he had seen
Moses! And Elijah! And they had spoken to him.

He was shouting about building houses—mansions—for
the two of them and a slightly smaller one for me.

I asked John what he had seen and he said, "I saw two
old men. You were talking with them and you were glowing."

I said, "Glowing?"

He said, "Glowing. But that's how I always see you.
What did you see?"

I said, "Well, I saw Moses first and he said to me, 'You?
Really, you?'"

"And I asked what he meant and he asked, 'How many plagues have you caused?'

"And I said none.

"Then he asked, 'How many of Pharaoh's charioteers have you killed?'

"And I said none.

"And he asked, 'How many followers do you have?'

"I said twelve, and he said, 'Twelve? Twelve? Really? I led a nation out of Egypt.'

"And I said, 'Yes, I know.' Then—'I'm sorry.'"

I sat up as I said to John, "Elijah asked me, 'How many local prophets have you killed?' and I said none.

"He asked, 'How do you get around?'

I said, 'I walk.'

"He asked, 'Where's your chariot of fire?'

"I answered, 'I don't have one and, yes,' I said, 'I know. I'm sorry.'

"And then I was surrounded by God.

"I felt I was inside God like being inside a mist or a storm and I said, 'I'm sorry. I'm sorry.'

"And God asked, 'For what?'

"'For being a disappointment.'"

"And God asked, 'What's *disappointment*?'

"I said, 'A feeling of failure.'

"And God said, 'I'm an expert in that.'

"'How can that be? You're perfect.'

"'Look around at the world. Do you think this is what I intended? Moses and Elijah causing plagues and killing prophets? I am a complete failure.'

"'What do you mean?'

"'Why do you think you feel me as a mist or a storm? That's as much of me as people are willing to understand.

Pillars of fire, yes. Burning bushes, yes. But they can't see me as a person. They are happier slaying prophets and causing plagues and other bloody things that have nothing to do with me.

"'I live in love—like the love John has for you—and love will always fail because it will always overreach. It will try everything and fall short. I need a prophet who can love so much that the prophecy must fail because it reaches beyond the possible.

"'Are you that prophet, my son?'

"I said, 'I have already failed. I brought Peter, James, and John up this mountain to tell them that I was disbanding the group because I had failed. I cannot complete the size of what I feel. I can't even find words to say it.'

"'Are you willing to keep trying until you fail completely?'

"'And that won't disappoint you?'

"'What's *disappointment*?'

"Then he said, 'After you fail finally, you will rise finally. Like all people who live to love.'

"And then he vanished."

And it was just me alone in John's arms.

And James trying to calm down Peter shouting about mansions.

The mansions would have to wait.

Do You Want an Angel?

"Now my soul is troubled. And what should I say—
'Father, save me from this hour'? No, it is for this reason
that I have come to this hour. Father, glorify your
name." Then a voice came from heaven, "I have
glorified it, and I will glorify it again." The crowd stand-
ing there heard it and said that it was thunder. Others
said, "An angel has spoken to him."

—John 12:27–29

What did you hear?

Did you hear thunder? Or an angel?

Hard call.

The answer says as much about you as it does about what happened.

You have to understand, I come from a family that was routinely visited by angels.

My mother tells me that I am here because an angel arrived in the middle of an ordinary day and told her that she was going to have a child. When the angel said she would have a child, my mother asked, "How?" And this stumped the angel. The angel said, "Pardon me?" My mother asked, "How will I have a child? I am unmarried and a virgin. How will this happen?"

When the angel was silent, my mother asked what was wrong.

The angel said, "Well, no one's ever asked me a question before. Usually I deliver a message; people are in awe of my presence; they fall to their knees; I go away. I never have to answer questions. I'm not entirely sure I can."

My mother said, "Well, sit down at the kitchen table while I'll make you a cup of tea. I am sure we can work this out." And they did and she said, "Fine. Be it done according to your will." They parted on good terms and here I am.

My mother was a very practical woman. I was always surprised that she would deal with angels, but she said angels are very practical beings. If you need to get something done fast, there's nothing more practical than an angel.

My father said that he saw angels in his dreams, but I'm not sure if I actually believed him. The best way to get my mother to do something was to tell her that an angel had given the order.

For myself, I think I saw angels in the desert. I think. It was forty days of fasting in extreme heat and terrible cold. I saw many inexplicable things, so I don't know if they were angels or hallucinations.

And now people are trying to kill me. There are plans in place to end my life. They are looking to frighten me. They have succeeded. I am terrified and confused and losing sleep. Under so much stress, my hair is falling out. I am trying to decide if I will go to Jerusalem and risk it or run away. So when Phillip and Andrew brought these Greeks to me— very nice men and women—seeking truth, I have no truth to give them.

I babble.

Trying to convince myself that death isn't so bad, I say, "A seed has to die to grow," but a person is not a seed and how does a person grow after death? I babble until my babble is interrupted by an enormous noise.

A tremendous crash that stuns us all.

People heard different things: Some people said it was an angel; others, thunder.

I asked the Greeks what they had heard.

They said, "You first. What did you hear?"

I said, "I heard thunder."

"Was that all?"

"No. In the thunder, I heard an angel speaking.

"And the angel—he or she I couldn't tell—was saying, Joshua son of Mary, I have a question for you."

I said. "I'm not used to having angels ask me questions."

"Well," he said, "let's work this out as your mother taught us both."

"Ask your question," I said.

He said, "People are plotting against you."

"Yes," I said.

And he—or she—asked, "Do you want an angel?"

I said, "Pardon me?"

She or he said, "Do you want a fiery chariot to take you away from this? Do you want an angel?"

Do I want an angel?

I said, "The first day of my ministry, I preached, 'blessed are the poor.'"

The angel said, "We were all there. We heard."

I asked, "Do the poor have angels to solve their problems?"

"No," the angel said. "We watch. We console. We do not solve."

"And on that day when I came down from the mountain, a leper asked me to heal him. I said that I wanted to but I didn't know if I could. I touched him. My touch changed him. Everyone saw that. But no one noticed how that touch changed me."

The angel said, "We noticed. I noticed."

"That touch was intimate. It joined us forever. I learned what could happen between two people. The intimacy of the healing touch." I asked, "Do angels have such touches?"

And the angel said, "No. Never."

I said, "Did you see the woman who came to me at dinner in the house of Simon the Pharisee? A woman making her living on the street? Crushed with shame, she crashed the dinner and poured perfume on my feet and kissed them."

And the angel said, "I saw."

"That intimacy? Do angels have such intimacy?"

And the angel said, "Never."

I said, "You saw the death of my father. How death increased the love between him and my mother almost unbearably. As if all the love of eternity had to be compressed into the sleepless nights when she took care of him."

And the angel said, "I saw."

I said, "Do angels have such love?"

The angel said, "No."

I repeated, "No?"

The angel said, "No."

"Well, then," I said, "no angels."

And he or she said, "Are you sure?"

I said, "No. Angels are always sure, aren't they. Humans never. Then I will be unsure with them. Intimate as they are. And I will die with them. I will compress an eternity of love into a few days. Into a meal. Into a cup. Onto a plate. And I will give them that."

The angel said, "Be it done according to thy will."

I smiled.

I explained this to the Greeks and asked what they had heard.

They said, "Well, we only heard thunder. But in your story of the leper, of the woman, of your father and mother—in your voice, we heard the voice of God."

As had I.

A Cure for Death

Then Jesus, again greatly disturbed, came to the tomb. It was a cave, and a stone was lying against it. Jesus said, "Take away the stone."... When he had said this, he cried with a loud voice, "Lazarus, come out!" The dead man came out, his hands and feet bound with strips of cloth, and his face wrapped in a cloth. Jesus said to them, "Unbind him, and let him go."

—John 11:38–44

I was Lazarus's best man.

I was a workingman; he was a member of a family that controlled a big part of the building trade. If times were slow in Nazareth and I heard of a major building project, I would pick up my tools and go where the work was. It's a three-day walk from Nazareth to Bethany, and there were many times I walked it for work.

Sometimes I found myself with Lazarus working beside me; not that I knew that he was the boss's son. All I knew was that he was a young man with bad work habits and very expensive tools. He was a bit of a danger to himself and, frankly, to the rest of us. I helped him learn the trade.

Lazarus had the ease and polish that come with wealth. Light seemed to bounce off him differently from the rest of us. The crew appreciated that he never condescended. He did his best. He learned and helped out as best he could. That's all anyone can ask.

We became close after he put down the tools—some of which he gave me—and started to manage worksites. He was a gifted manager.

When he'd come to visit me in Nazareth, he would bring expensive presents for my mother. Eventually she told him to stop, which he appreciated. At my house, Lazarus was valued for himself.

When he would leave, my mother would say to me, "A rich man getting into heaven would be like squeezing a camel through the eye of a needle."

I would reply, "That's the dumbest metaphor I have ever heard."

She would say, "Wait and see."

When he stayed with us, we slept in the same bed, as was the custom, and talked late into the night. We would wake in one another's arms. We were brothers. I became close to his sisters. Mary was a teacher of a discipline from the East called yoga, and Martha worked with her father on the interior design of buildings.

One night, late, he asked me how he would know if he was in love. I told him his body would fill with light. He said, "In that case, I'm in love."

I was his best man, as he was supposed to be mine.

I was his best man, but he didn't marry the woman he loved.

He married the woman his father wanted him to marry for the sake of the business.

He and Lizabeth had reasonable expectations of one another: comfort, security, and children.

Over time, each felt cheated by the other.

Not financially. The money piled up. The more they had, the less they enjoyed it. After his father died, Lazarus worked feverishly growing the business. He saw less and less of Lizabeth or the children and whatever light had been in him faded.

When I turned thirty, Lazarus was the first person I asked to join me in my new work. The very first. I thought it would give him a new start and add some respectability to my preaching to have a rich man as a disciple. I said, "Give it all up. You have plenty. You're rich. You can retire. You never have to work again."

He turned me down. He said Lizabeth and the children needed him to work.

I said, "They barely see you. You are working yourself to an early grave. Where has the light gone, Lazarus?"

He blew up at me and said things that I hoped he would later regret.

"Look at you," he said. "You've got nothing. You're a homeless beggar. You never even got married. What's your problem, Joshua? Look at where the two of us are and then tell me: Who has betrayed the light?"

I began to think that my mother had been right about the camel.

Not that I told her.

Three years later, when I heard that he was sick—his sisters had sent word—I didn't go to see him. I knew what "sick" meant. He was depressed. The last person he would want to see was me, since my star was in the ascendant.

I finally went when I got word my friend had died.

When I arrived at the house, there was extraordinary weeping and wailing—the kind of crying that doesn't come just for a death but for the death of someone who left a great deal of the serious work of life undone.

I didn't know if I could do what I was hoping I could do.

I was tired and miracles frequently didn't work when I was tired.

I stood in front of the cave.

I shouted into the darkness.

I shouted, "Lazarus, come forth!"

People looked at me as if I had lost my mind.

I wept. I shouted, "Lazarus, come forth!"

I knew I was tempting God as I had once before.

That time I had failed.

Still I shouted, "You've been in a cave too many years, friend. Come out! Come out! My brother, come out!"

Martha, his sister, was the first to shout with me. I wasn't expecting it. She actually frightened me with her roar. She shouted, "Come forth, brother! Come forth!"

Mary joined her in a higher key.

And his children.

Before long all of us—actually, not all, but most (some just looked at us as if we were mad)—most of us were shouting, bellowing, sobbing, "Lazarus, come forth!"

Not Lizabeth.

Not for a long time.

Then the cry exploded out of her.

"Husband, come out! Come to me!"

And he came out.

We slept together in the same bed again that night.

Now grown men.

He asked, "How did you do that?"

I asked, "What happened?"

He said, "You know I hanged myself."

I said, "I assumed."

"At the construction site. I didn't want the family to find me.... Death isn't the end," he said.

"I know," I said.

"I sat in the cold and the dark. I'd like to say I was more alone than I ever had been before, but that's not true. It was just more of the same—only there was no work to distract me from the darkness."

"And then," I said hopefully, "you saw the light?"

He shook his head no.

"There was no light. I felt the darkness. The unspeakable depth of the darkness. And I thought, yes, finally. I can just give in to it. Disappear into the darkness.... Then you called."

"And then," I said, "you saw the light?"

He shook his head no.

He said, "I wanted to shout at you, 'Leave me alone! Leave me where I deserve to be!'"

"And *then* you saw the light?"

"I told you," he said, "There was no light. I saw darkness. Not just my own. I saw the darkness that I had placed in my children by not loving them. I could feel the darkness inside my sisters on whom I had turned my back. Above all... above all, I could feel my wife's hope that she would someday find someone who would love her.... And I wanted to be that man desperately. Then—more frightened of life than death—I came out. The call was irresistible. I didn't see any light until I came out and saw them—and you. And *then* light filled my body."

I held him as he cried.

We were silent.

Lazarus finally said, "I will follow you now. If you can cause this to happen, I will follow you."

"Too late," I said. "My journey is about to come to an end. Now that I have done this, they will need me dead. Your work is here. Fill your house. Fill it with light. Be the light of your house. But I do have a favor to ask of you."

"Ask," he said.

"When I die..."

"Don't even think of it," he said. "You are the one necessary person alive."

"When I die, wait by my tomb. Bring your sisters and your family. Bring the builders we were friends with. Bring everyone you know. Come with the disciples. And the women.

"And stand there.

"And call my name. Call me forth. Call me back into the light.

"Remember to stand at the tomb and call my name.

"Don't leave me in the darkness."

He said, "I don't have your power."

I said, "I called you, yes. But you didn't come out until your wife called. Who knows what miracles remain in us undone?"

Lazarus looked at me as if I were mad.

Still, I thought... if not Lazarus, who had been called from death, who would come to call for me?

Gladius

But after his brothers had gone to the festival, then he also went, not publicly but as it were in secret. The Jews were looking for him at the festival and saying, "Where is he?" And there was considerable complaining about him among the crowds. While some were saying, "He is a good man," others were saying, "No, he is deceiving the crowd." Yet no one would speak openly about him for fear of the Jews. About the middle of the festival Jesus went up into the temple and began to teach.

—John 7:10–14

I have an authority problem.

You see, I feel I have it. Direct from God. This creates problems, but I have another authority problem now. I have lost contact with my inner authority. I have lost my connection with God. I have lost the plot. And I am frightened.

I sent the disciples up to Jerusalem to celebrate the Feast of Booths and I stayed behind, quaking in my sandals.

But now that I am by myself, I find the thought that has been tormenting me laughable. I am not important enough that the temple leadership would be plotting my death. And yet...

Every time I take a step toward Jerusalem, my knees give out from under me and I fall. Yet I know a task awaits me there, though I don't know what. And I will never know unless I go.

When I can put up with my cowardice no longer, I decide to go to the feast in disguise. I make my cloak into a hood and go up to the feast.

I mingle. I blend in. I am invisible.

Being invisible, I begin to relax.

It becomes clear to me that I am crazy, paranoid, and that everything is fine.

I decide to enjoy the feast.

I look for a cook in the market and buy some braised lamb from her. I ask, "What about that nice Joshua man who's been going around healing people? Is he at the feast?" And she says, "Not that I've seen." I say, "Well, that's a shame." And she says, "Not really, love. If he shows his face around here, they'll kill him as soon as look at him . . . Here's your lamb, love."

And my knees grow weak.

I find a leper begging at the edge of the crowd. I give him the lamb and ask, "Is Joshua here? He might cure you, you know." And he says to me, "If you see him before I do, tell him to hide."

The child I ask says, "If he's hiding, they must be right in what they say about him. He wouldn't be hiding if he didn't have something to hide. That's what my father says."

I know now that this must be dealt with. I'm not the type who can live in hiding.

I find myself standing in the middle of the temple shouting, "Here I am. Come and get me if you want me. Why are you trying to kill me?"

When the authorities shout back that I am insane and no one is trying to kill me, the people laugh.

I shout to the crowd. "Am I talking to my killer? Is it one of you? Are you here? How will you do it? Stab me in a dark alley? Push me off a cliff? Make yourself known! Maybe I can talk you out of it."

A man shouts back, "That's not how it works, Joshua. They won't hire a killer. There would be paperwork. A trail that could be used against them."

"So how does it work then?" I ask.

"There is a price on your head. Whosoever kills you can claim the prize, and no one will have to admit to plotting your death."

"How much?"

"You don't want to advertise that," shouted a woman. "Everyone will become a potential assassin if the price is right." And there is laughter.

I say, "Come on then. Tell me."

"Thirty pieces of silver," another man shouts. "If they go up another ten, I'm thinking of taking it myself." And everyone laughs. "But I think you are safe here with us, hiding in plain sight."

"You're not safe actually," comes a darker voice from the shadows. "Because it's not enough for them that you die. You must be seen to be punished. You must be seen to be abandoned by God."

That silences the crowd.

"And how will they make that happen?" I ask.

He answers, "The Romans. They will find a way to give you to the Romans so that they can execute you."

This terrifies me. All confidence drops out of me. I almost collapse.

There is a Roman centurion with several soldiers in the temple to keep order. All eyes go to him. Our eyes meet. In his eyes, I see complete authority.

I say to the crowd, "They wouldn't be so cruel."

The man in the shadows replies, "Oh wouldn't they? You have challenged their temple."

I say, "Your hearts are the temple of God. I worship there. I wish to be with you."

Then I shout to the authorities, "Don't take me away from the people I love! Don't treat me in death as if I were a stranger. The Romans execute to terrorize. Don't make me an object of terror. Don't use me to frighten the people into obedience. Don't do that. You can't be that cruel."

Then I shout to the centurion. I say, "You know me."

He looks at me blankly. "Do I?" he asks.

I say, "You do. Would you stand between me and harm?"

And he shouts back, "And why would I do that?"

I say, "I saved the life of your servant."

People wait to hear what a centurion indebted to a Jew will say.

And he says, "I remember you now. You said at the time that it was my faith that saved him, didn't you? And I have this to tell you. If ordered, I would do the job myself. And they could keep their silver. My wages are good enough. It's what I am paid to do. Now break this up. Move along. The show is over."

And we are left alone, the centurion and I.

He says, "Come with me."

I follow him down a dark, empty passageway.

When we are out of the sight of the crowd, he puts me up against a wall and takes his sword from its scabbard, holds it up to me, and I think, well, this is it.

A foolish death.

So be it.

He speaks with passion, "Do you see this? This is a good Roman sword. Made from a single piece of carbon steel. Forged in white-hot flame. A Roman *gladius*. Centuries of war have shaped it into a perfect instrument for fighting. Look, the sides can be used for cutting, but the point is sharp for stabbing. Feel it. It has a good solid hilt with ridges for the fingers."

He places the sword in my hand. When I try to hand it back, he says urgently, quietly, "Take it. Keep it close to you, friend. Use it if you need to. And never ask me to acknowledge you in public again. You should know better."

He starts to turn away.

I say, "I could never kill a man, even if he were coming to kill me."

Turning back, he says, "Do you think I don't know that? That's not why I am giving it to you.

"If it comes to that—and I pray the gods it doesn't—I am urging you to die like a Roman. Fall on your sword. I will show you how. Place the point here, up under the ribs. When you fall, you will drive the sword into your heart. It's an honorable death. And quick. And you deprive your enemy of his victory. You deprive them of their power. They will have no victory over you."

I feel the weight of the sword...and its meaning to him...and its meaning to me.

I feel his absolute authority and I want to gain strength from it. But the strength comes from somewhere else.

I look at the sword and say, "You're right. This is a good Roman sword. So much work has gone on through the ages to make it into the perfect weapon."

He nodds.

"And look at you, soldier. How hard they must have worked to make you what you are. Like the sword, a beautiful weapon. All polished brass and worn leather. How cruel they must have been to you. Forced marches. Starving you. Beating you...."

He says, "Pissing on us too."

"How many sleepless nights did they make you endure to turn you into another perfect weapon? And how sad for them—after all that effort—that they haven't succeeded."

He says, "Don't mistake who I am. I am a Roman soldier."

I smile as strength returns.

"And here you are, Roman centurion, giving me the most prized possession of a soldier: the sword that you worked so hard to earn. What trouble you'd be in if your superiors knew that you were giving a weapon to an insurgent. What would happen if they caught you giving your sword to a religious fanatic?"

"I would be beaten to death by my own men."

He says this without pity for himself.

"How good you are to give me this to spare me pain."

I offer him the sword back. He declines.

"Perhaps," he says, "I am giving it to you to spare myself pain."

"I don't think so," I say. "You're inured to pain. I was once impressed with your faith. Now I am overwhelmed by your love. Talking to you has restored me to myself. You have restored my faith in God."

"The gods," he said, "are ridiculous."

"Well," I say, "your gods certainly are. And perhaps our War God is ridiculous too. But this—this that is happening between us here, now—this, to me, is God. This truly useless act of absolute generosity—this is God."

"Well, then," he says, "God is a very weak and useless thing."

"Still," I say, "enough to bring your servant back to life."

"Are you counting on that for yourself?" he asks.

I say, "Well, you see, I have this authority problem. I feel I can never be separated from him."

I hand him back his sword.

He says, "I hope I never see you again. But, if I do, I will try to make your suffering as short as possible."

And I say, "Friend, you already have."

And I walk back into the temple and turn over the tables of the moneychangers.

The Last Supper

*"This is my commandment, that you love one another as
I have loved you. No one has greater love than this, to
lay down one's life for one's friends. You are my friends
if you do what I command you."*

—John 15:12–14

There wasn't as much sitting as you might think.

In fact, was there ever a moment when all of us were at
the table at the same time?

I don't recall.

The children under the table were distracting.

The women serving were fighting with the men.

There was way too much drinking, because of which all
the disciples would fall asleep when I needed them most.

People were moving around constantly.

I was moving around constantly: washing feet, filling
cups, serving food.

The whole thing was chaotic and disturbing.

I spoke pages of thoughts but never to the whole group.
The whole group was impossible to address. I spoke to small
groups as I moved up and down the table trying to relieve my
anxiety about the coming catastrophe. Who knows? Perhaps
my anxiety was why the disciples were drinking so heavily.

When I tried to get some control over the group, I inadvertently started a fight. I asked, "Do you know the ten commandments?" and they began to try to list them in order, as if it were a drinking game.

God. Swearing. Sabbath. Parents. Kill. Adultery. Steal. False witness. Covet. Covet. Covet.

Philip said, "Did any of you ever notice that the commandment after 'Honor your father and mother' is 'Thou shalt not kill'? A coincidence? I don't think so."

Amid the laughter, I said, "I have a new commandment for you. Love one another."

That quieted the group.

"Love one another."

Someone said, "Just that?"

I said, "Yes. Just that."

Others said, "What about all the healings and curing...?"

"And caring for the poor and...?"

"What about all the parables that we didn't understand?"

"What about...."

My voice shook as I said again, perhaps with an unwanted edge of anger, "Love one another. Be what we have always been. Friends."

"Friends?" one of them called out. "Since when are we your friends?"

When they saw that this puzzled me, they explained, "We have always been your disciples. Followers. Students. And slow students, as you have always reminded us. When did we become friends?"

I didn't know what to say.

Could I somehow have forgotten to call them friends all this time?

Had I been so busy teaching them lessons of justice that I had forgotten to love them?

Was it too late to start now?

What had I done?

Worse! What had I left undone?

A child crawled out from under the table and took my hand. She said to them, "He's trembling."

Out of the silence that had descended on the room John stood up and put a hand on my heart.

He said to the others, "Thunder."

The others came up one by one, put hands on me and embraced me until we were standing together as a group holding one another.

I took advantage of the silence and spoke as quickly as I could.

I said, "This is my commandment: love one another as I love you. No one has greater love than this, to lay down one's life for one's friends. I call you friends. I ask you—I command you, if a friend can command—love one another—if love can be commanded...."

Magdalene started a song. I think she began it to stop me from saying any more. There was no more to be said.

They all took it up and together we walked out into the night.

Only Magdalene remained.

Magdalene said, "I always knew."

I said, "I know."

She took my hand, and we walked out together.

She did not fall asleep that night.

The Story of a Kiss

Now the betrayer had given them a sign, saying, "The one I will kiss is the man; seize him and lead him away under guard." And when he came, he went up to him at once, and said, "Master!" And he kissed him.

—Mark 14:44–45

Why a kiss?

A kiss?

He could have done it with a nod of his head.

Less.

A glance would have done it.

He could have met the centurion's eyes with his. The centurion's look would have asked. "Which one?" A quick glance at me and back to the Roman—done. He could have accomplished that from within the safety of the pack of apostles. But no. He wanted me to know it was him.

Did he want me to know more than that?

Why the kiss?

We had fought about kisses a few days earlier.

He had objected when a working woman ran into Simon the Pharisee's house where we were having dinner. She dropped to her knees in front of me, crying so hard I had to ask for a towel to dry myself off.

Costly tears.

She had sworn that she would never love another man, and yet here she was expressing love she had resolved never to feel again.

She kissed me.

She couldn't stop.

I thanked her for her kisses.

I told her I needed them.

When Judas objected, I explained that these innocent kisses might be the last ones I would ever have before my death.

Now, he kissed me.

His was the last kiss.

And this was not a casual kiss on the cheek.

His lips embraced my lips.

He took my head in his hands and held me in the kiss.

The contact was long; long enough to have a story to it.

This kiss could have spoken of friendship, had it not become passionate.

The passion could have been love, until it became aggressive.

The aggression became anger.

The anger, punishing.

Kisses challenge the thin boundary that separates us.

Sometimes this is love; sometimes not.

The boundary between us broke.

He broke into the source of my love as if he were trying to steal it.

It was pleasure misused.

I do not remember who ended it. Did he step back? Did I push him away? In the storm of physical responses—shock, pleasure, arousal, fear—details escape me.

All I could say was, "Why a kiss?"

He responded, "How can you ask?"

I said, "But why betray with a kiss?"

Looking into my memory of his eyes, I now see answers I did not see in the few seconds that remained to us.

His eyes said. "How can you not understand?

"How can you not know that kisses aren't always innocent?

"Or desired?

"Are you now frightened by a kiss as I was once?

"Many times more than once.

"Do you understand now the betrayal I have felt for most of my life?

"Can you feel what I feel every day when you talk about that terrifying thing that is love?

"Why the father covering the son with prodigal kisses on his return is terrifying to me?

"Why I need to run from love when it is offered?

"Why I need to not trust your love?

"Do you see?

"Do you see now why this must be done with a kiss?"

I am sure that later they will say he did it for the money.

It was never the money.

Some will understand; most will not.

And those who understand will probably not be able to find the words to explain. Or be frightened enough of their own understanding that they will settle for the simpler explanation. Of course, it was for the money because it is too frightening to think what he had suffered.

Those who understand will know he was not turning his back on me.

He was trying to make me understand what cannot be understood if not experienced.

I have healed many people of many diseases, but always—always—I have had to feel the pain of the person suffering, and I would have been incapable of understanding this pain.

Until now.

Now, because of that kiss, my body will be used for others' enjoyment.

My body will now be subjected to the sick pleasure of others.

Now I will feel what you felt.

Betrayal.

Stripping.

Confinement.

Penetration.

I will learn to understand.

Forgive me for not understanding before.

I will learn.

But now you, Judas, you will learn too.

You have betrayed me with a kiss, and now you will learn what it is to abuse.

And this will be a hard learning, for—despite this brutal act—you are a gentle soul and, with that kiss, the boundary between us broke in both directions.

I suspect you felt my love.

A love that you too swore you would never feel again.

And tears will be shed.

Tears enough for many towels.

I ask you to remain in my love.

I will come back.

I will come back to you.

I will come back for you.

I will find the way somehow.

Till then, live in my love.

Live.

Until one kiss can be redeemed by another.

Anna, Daughter of Phanuel

There was also a prophet, Anna the daughter of
Phanuel, of the tribe of Asher. She was of a great age,
having lived with her husband seven years after her
marriage, then as a widow to the age of eighty-four. She
never left the temple but worshiped there with fasting
and prayer night and day. At that moment she came,
and began to praise God and to speak about the child to
all who were looking for the redemption of Jerusalem.
—Luke 2:36–38

It's strange—making a life-and-death decision. You don't add up the pluses and minuses like you might for a lesser decision. Your mind chooses a moment, maybe an insignificant one, because all the important moments are defined by the small ones that have come before, aren't they?

Now I am facing a life-and-death choice and, absurdly, I am seeing myself as a child—maybe ten, maybe a bit older—at the table in the kitchen, annoying my mother as she prepares dinner. I had run into the kitchen and, out of nowhere, shouted to my mother, "I want to live to be a hundred."

Still working, she said, "Why a hundred?"

I answered, "I love being alive."

She said, "No. Why stop at a hundred?"

She never stopped working or even looked up as we spoke.

I told her that I thought a hundred was as far as a person could go.

She said, while chopping chickpeas, "I once knew a woman who was 104. Her name was Anna, daughter of Phanuel, and she lied about her age. She said she was 84, but she was actually twenty years older."

I asked, "Why would she lie about her age? I'd think she'd be proud."

My mother said, "Wait till you're forty. You'll understand."

I was liking this conversation, so I sat down and asked, "How old did she live to?"

My mother said she didn't know—she had met her only once—the day I was given my name—and it was time for her to get her work done and I should go away and the conversation ended.

That night as she put me to bed, I asked my mother to finish the story.

She said, "Why do you want to hear old stories?"

I said I didn't want to hear all the old stories, just the ones that were about me.

She said fine and, as she turned down my bed, she told me about that day.

"Anna was a prophetess at the temple when your father and I took you there to be circumcised and named.

"There were many men there that day—priests and mohels and deacons—so many men. And only one woman: Anna, daughter of Phanuel. I was young, fourteen, and frightened by the men. Anna saw that, and she came to stand by my side and comfort me.

"I started to compliment her and she said, 'I know, I know, I am an attractive woman for eighty-four.'"

My mother said that wasn't what she was going to say. She was going to say that she, Anna, was beautiful at any age.

Anna laughed and said, "Well," she said. "Then I'll tell you my real age. I am 104. And even now, after 104 years, they still call me Anna, *daughter of Phanuel*! Maybe someone will see me as just *Anna* some day."

"Then," my mother said to me, "she looked at you and said, 'That's a beautiful child.'"

"Was I?" I asked.

My mother said to me what she said to Anna, "All babies are beautiful."

Anna laughed and sighed, "Well, I've seen more babies than you have, but yours is a beautiful child. I am a prophetess. Do you wish me to tell you his future?"

This, even when I was a child, frightened me.

My mother said, "No. But pray for him."

Anna said, "Shall I pray for a long life for him?"

I was hoping my mother had said yes, but what she said was, "Is long life good?"

Anna answered thoughtfully, "You're the first mother ever to ask that.

"Age? It can be hard. I have outlived my husband by sixty years. More. I have outlived most of my children. And some of their children as well. And I am enjoying their children.

"So age has its blessings as well. You cease to be afraid of death. Because you have seen so much of it, you realize that death is inconsequential. It matters less than you would think when you can see the grand sweep of things. It's what your life reveals that matters."

My mother asked, "What will my son's life reveal?"

Anna, whispering, said, "Do you know what's inside this child? Deep inside?"

My mother waited.

"Anna took you in her arms and she said, 'God.'

"She said, 'God. God is inside. The priests think God is in the holy of holies. Ha! Fooled them. God is in here as in every child. Yes, you can see that in his eyes even now. Such wonder.

'But it's up to the mother what the child will reveal.

'Want him to be too successful and he will forget the God within. Punish him too severely and he will become angry and closed. Don't punish him at all? He will become unruly. It's a very delicate thing...

'And your embrace. It can't be too tight or too loose...

'You must let him become everything that is in him. People are afraid of their own tenderness for one another. Their own fierceness at injustice. People grow afraid of their own truth...

'And you can't want him to be like anyone else. You must let him become himself, because that is God's truth. An imitation of no one. A revelation in himself...

'Above all, listen to what is unique in him. His particular joys; his particular sorrows. Coax his particular gifts into their fullness and God will be revealed whether his life is long or short."

My mother said, "Then pray for that. That he might know his own truth and become it."

The prophetess said, "It's a hard road."

My mother said, "It's the only road I know."

"And that," my mother said to me, "is what she prayed for you.

"That was the last time I saw her. I said, 'Farewell, Anna. *Just* Anna.' She laughed. And she blessed me as well, and we went home. End of story. Go to sleep."

I asked my mother, "Have I become true? Is God revealed in me?"

And she said, "Some days I think so."

I said, "The days when I am good."

She said, "No. Usually not. When you are unexpected. Laugh for no reason. Say, out of nowhere, that you want to be a hundred. Hug me without cause. Know when your father is lonely and step into his arms. . . . You're like God then. Besides, I don't think anyone can tell you if God is revealed in you. You have to know that in yourself. . . . Anna knew it of herself. The child was still alive in her. Full of wonder and passion. And that's what made her beautiful."

And here I am—twenty years later—and a life-and-death question is being asked me.

Pilate has asked me a question.

He has asked, "Are you a king?"

What am I to tell him?

I know if I say no, it's all been a terrible mistake, I will walk out that door. He will probably even find me useable. Hire me. And I will have a long life.

All I have to do is say I am not what I am.

And I stand here thinking—strangely thinking—of Anna, a woman I never met and her prayer for me.

And her faith that God was within me waiting to be revealed.

And I hear Anna saying "Death? Death is inconsequential. Truth matters. God is revealed."

And I find myself saying, unexpectedly even to myself, "I am a king. For this I was born and for this I have come into the world, to bear witness to the truth. Everyone who is of the truth hears my voice."

And as I say it, I hear my mother's voice asking the prophetess to pray for me.

And I hear Anna's prayer.

And I know, even if I have failed in every other way, at least I have been the answer to an old woman's prayer.

And I know I will not see 104.

Or 100.

Or 84.

Or even 40.

And I know—without question—that Anna's prayer is fulfilled in me.

The Map Back

Early on the first day of the week, while it was still dark,
Mary Magdalene came to the tomb and saw that the
stone had been removed from the tomb.

—John 20:1

Yes, a voice did ask, "Why do you seek the living among the dead?" But it wasn't an angel who spoke. And I didn't hear it from the tomb where, to console themselves, they insist I was laid. They wrote a lot about my execution and what happened after. But they weren't there. They didn't know. They wrote anyway. She knew. But she couldn't write.

They didn't listen to her. Or perhaps they couldn't. Resurrection is a language. To some, she could teach it, but it's a costly learning and they were wedded to Greek. Aramaic. Paper. Ink. They weren't yet speaking resurrection that is written in blood and flesh and spirit and death. And once you have learned it, you realize how laughably insufficient paper and ink and words—even these words—are.

"Father forgive them for they know not what they do"? I didn't say that. That's what they needed to hear me say. But you don't make conversation on the cross. When your tendons are ripping from your bones, you have no thought for speech. You are drawing a map in your brain—a map that you knew as a child. When you are a child, you hold your hands in front of your eyes wondering whose they are. You put your foot in your mouth to learn it is part of you. These things are yours. More, they are you. And all the while you are drawing a map of your body.

On the cross, that map is torn up. The nails in your hands and feet tell you your hands and feet are not your own. You are told by the whip your skin is not your own. They drain the blood from your body to show you it is theirs to take. As this is happening, you desperately try to redraw the map. To find some way to reclaim your first and last possession as your own. That was the battle I was fighting on the cross. Could I remain my own? I wasn't thinking of forgiveness. I wasn't thinking at all.

She was there to see most of it, but they forced her and the others away at the end. They wanted no fight over the body. Even so, there was a skirmish. I heard it from the ground they laid me on. After death, a rudimentary consciousness remains, though, at the time, I didn't know how.

The skirmish was over my body. A man demanded it. He had paid good money for it, he said. But the centurion said Pilate may have taken the bribe, but the body was not to be honored. No one who said he was a king could have a tomb around which the credulous could create a myth. When violence threatened, the fight ended. The man was committed to me, but not to the point of risking death. He was not her.

The soldier picked me up. My body remembers this. He hoisted me easily over his shoulder. My body remembers even now the shape of his shoulder in my abdomen as he walked to the cart on which the bodies of the crucified were placed. When we arrived at the pit—a long journey—he defied his orders to bury me deep in the bodies. Instead, he threw me. A bloodless body is light. He lifted me high and threw me into the middle of the pit where I landed among the dead and felt every death going back to Adam. They said to me, "So you have come to free us after all?" I asked, "How can I do that when I am with you in the pit?" And they said, "How could you do it if you weren't with us in the pit?"

Decomposition is more frightening than death. You strain to hold the torn map together knowing there will come a point at which your body and its consciousness of itself dissolves. "Find me" is the panicked cry that comes out of you. Or came out of me at least. "Don't let me be lost. Find me. Preserve me," were the only words I had. I did not yet speak resurrection.

She was looking. Or trying to look.

There was chaos in the streets. A storm—an earthquake—political turmoil. Chaos forced her to stay inside.

When she could escape, she ran to Joseph of Arimathea, who had fought the centurion for my body and lost. When he told her that their plans for my burial in his tomb had been circumvented, she went mad. She bolted to the tomb, which was of course empty, with the burial clothes folded neatly in the corner, just as she had prepared them for me. They would use that later for proof of my rising, but you can't prove with cloth what has happened in flesh. She ran to the Roman barracks to find out what they did with the bodies of the executed. They mocked her, but her madness frightened them into telling her the location and she ran to the place everyone else avoided. The Pit.

It was then that I heard, "Why do you seek the living among the dead?" They got that right. But it wasn't an angel who spoke. It was a Roman soldier standing at the lip of the pit, gathering his courage to descend into it and pour lime on the bodies as he had been ordered to do. He couldn't do it, so he was amazed when she climbed into the pit without hesitation.

Everything in me wanted to shout, "I am here," but I did not yet know the language. Once in the pit, she hesitated among the dead, confused by the profusion of bodies. As I said, I had been hurled far into the pit, so I was not the first body she looked at. She took her time, and rightly so. We were all more than a little alike. All men. Mostly my age. The wounds that would distinguish me later did not distinguish me here. They were the one thing we all had in common. When I realized it was possible that she might not recognize me, I panicked. No, I despaired. My spirit shouted, "Here. I am here. Find me. Come for me. Comfort me. Hold me." But I was learning a new language. Making a new map.

The men later would be impressed that I could enter a locked room, which is nothing but a magician's trick. At this moment, I discovered I could enter a locked heart. Her heart was locked hard with rage. But I could bypass the rage and arrive at the center of her being, where I found myself filling her heart. Completely. Which humbled me. I had given Magdalene a portion of my attention—a share of my love. But inside her heart, I could feel that she had given me all of hers. Unreservedly. She had uprooted her life to follow me. I could feel the mockery she had endured for following a man who barely noticed her. Who wouldn't marry her. The mockery of the men who were the chosen as she was not. Rage at them. Rage at Judas. Rage at Peter. Rage at the Romans. Even rage at me. But within her—

Within her, I was whole. Preserved perfectly. Though not preserved. Alive within her. Every word. Every gesture. Every step of every journey. Perfect. From the first healing of the leper to the last sip of wine at the last supper. Every word was spoken again. All at once, yet each perfectly clear. The tone of voice. The inflection. I was safe within her. She was the tomb in which I was buried. The place from which

I still lived. Where I breathed. Where I grew into a new self. I could see myself within her. But I could also see her from within myself. See her quite objectively through my own closed eyes. I was learning the language. The language of eternal life. God's words.

Before we are born, we are carried contained within another. Completely. If someone had told you at the time that there were people waiting for you, you would have called them foolish. But we are carried until we can stand on our own. It is the same after death. I was being carried until I could stand. But language fails. Resurrection is written not with words—not even these words—but in body and blood, in spirit and, yes, excrement. Life stripped bare is eternal. Stripped of time. Stripped of barriers. Stripped of separation. And life now was utterly bare. With the strength of her rage, she cast aside body after body, searching for mine.

Then she stopped. She had found me. She wept. She wiped her tears that fell on my face. She took out oils, ointment, her best linen. She washed away the stains, the blood, the spit, the dirt, the excrement. She poured oil in my wounds. She kissed me and my heart broke because the body she was cherishing—that body was not mine. She had taken another discarded corpse for mine.

Everything in me wanted to shout—"No! Not him! Find me! Me! Leave him! Find me!"

I am glad I did not yet have the words because, at that moment, I began to learn the brutal lesson of resurrection.

I thought resurrection would be something for me. Mine. My victory. I had always felt that the rising would be a personal triumph for me. It's not. It's one more thing to be given. Given away. As freely as I had given my body and my blood—my resurrection was to be given away.

I had preached many times that what was done to the least of these was done to me—but, as long as I was preaching it, I was there. All eyes were on me. Now, no one saw me. No one. And then I truly died, because that's what it is to be dead finally. The world goes on without you. Now I was forced, not to just believe my own words, but to experience them.

Her love was not for me alone. That body, that thief, was also the son of God. That and any other body she might have mistakenly lavished her love on. All of them. I restrained my urge to cry out my name as long as I could. And the longer I waited, the more I realized that what the nails could not take from me, what the whip could not strip me of, what could not be drained from me, could be freely given.

The child's map was wrong.

Nothing is mine. Even what I fought on the cross to hold on to. It was all God's from the start.

It all could be given away.

I could feel warmth enter me.

I was learning resurrection.

Not only was the-least-of-these me, I was also him. My body was his, yes, but his was also mine. Her caresses of him, I began to feel myself. The map of my body was being redrawn again. The tenderness that I so envied being lavished on him was also being lavished on my body.

My body warmed to the warmth of her touch.

Slowly, stripped of ego, stripped even of self, finally stripped of everything that held me down in life, I rose.

A word escaped me. One word. A name. But not mine. Mary, I said.

She turned when she heard her name. At first, I couldn't tell if she could see me. Perhaps she couldn't tell either. Others would learn to see me, but for each one of them it took time. Some took hours. Some years. Some required proof.

Not Magdalene. She saw me not just with her eyes but with her whole self, and there was no question that she saw me. Then, in the next moment, she had a choice. To believe she was going mad or to believe in—not me—herself. Her experience. Her vision of me. An impossible seeing.

She ran toward me. She held me in her gaze and wouldn't look away, as if she was afraid I might vanish if she looked away. And perhaps I might have. I did not know the rules yet.

As she approached. I said, "Don't touch me." I was still afraid of pain. There was no more pain, but I didn't know that yet. I wish I had known then what I knew by the time I could say to Thomas, "Reach within me and know I am real." I wish I had said that to her.

I don't know if our words were spoken aloud or within us. The word "teacher" was spoken between us. But we both spoke it at the same moment, and each of us meant the other.

Then I annoyed her by asking her to tell the men I was alive. She said, "The men? Why? They ran."

I pointed to the bodies.

"There are so many to care for. Take the man you mistook for me."

She was puzzled.

She said, "I didn't mistake him. I know him. He was a gardener. And I knew you would want me to care for him, wouldn't you?"

I said, "Of course."

Then she ran away, filled with joy.

And when she had gone, the dead sat up and looked to me with a question.

"Will you leave us here?"

"No," I said, "it's for you I have come. This resurrection is yours. I know the way now. I have been given the map."

The Beauty of the City

*When they had gone ashore, they saw a charcoal fire
there, with fish on it, and bread. Jesus said to them,
"Bring some of the fish that you have just caught." So
Simon Peter went aboard and hauled the net ashore,
full of large fish, a hundred fifty-three of them; and
though there were so many, the net was not torn. Jesus
said to them, "Come and have breakfast."*

—John 21:9–12

She came up beside me in the street.

She slipped her hand into mine—like a younger child
than she was might do. I asked if she was lost. She said, "No.
I have been following you for some time now. Why are you
crying?"

I said, "I have been crying about the city."

"Are you crying," she asked, "because the city is so ugly?"

I nodded and said, "Yes. And so beautiful." I added, "I remember the first time I saw the city. I was a child. Your age."

The girl must have been twelve or thirteen.

"My parents brought me here and I didn't want to leave,
no matter what. I found a way to stay behind. They were
angry but I loved the city. It was the biggest and most beautiful thing I had ever seen."

"It can be beautiful," she said. "It is big."

I said, "It will look smaller to you when you get older. Every year it looks smaller to me. Now it looks very small. When I was thirty, I climbed to the top of the tower in the temple. I was thinking of jumping off."

She said, "My mother says the devil makes people do that."

"Perhaps," I said. "But I didn't jump. I loved what I saw. I was saved by the beauty of the city. I preached about it. The city on the hill cannot be hidden. I wanted to transform the city. I preached. I did miracles. We fought. We struggled. But I didn't transform it."

"The city welcomed you on Sunday," she said.

"You saw that, did you?"

"Oh, yes," she said. "People running and crying, 'Blessed is he who comes in the name of the Lord.' Oh, yes. I was shouting that too. I've seen you do many things. I've seen you cure people. I've heard your beautiful words. But how . . . how are you here?"

"What do you mean?" I asked. And she said, "It's impossible that you are here in these streets. It's impossible. I saw you die."

She said it again.

"I saw you die."

"Oh, yes," I said. "I remember that now . . .

"I wonder now if I should have jumped. I wonder if anything that happened in the three years between then and now was of value. Did I do anything worth doing, I wonder? I mean, what can anyone do? There is so much to do."

She was astounded and said, "Did you . . . ? Did you do anything? You must have. You're here. Though people don't seem to be noticing. How can they not notice you? I want to shout and tell them. Look. He's here. Behold. How can people be ignoring you?"

THE DIARY OF JESUS CHRIST

I shrugged and said, "This is new to me. I'm just starting to understand the rules...

"Perhaps I'm here because I didn't get done what needed to be done. Perhaps this is my second chance. I've learned a great deal. Death is quite a learning experience."

She asked, "What did you learn?"

"How kind of you to ask," I said. "No one is asking me questions these days, and I need help understanding what is happening."

We looked at one another.

She smiled. I smiled. I said, "I know you, don't I?" She nodded. "We met once," she said.

"When?"

She was disappointed I didn't remember her.

"Remind me," I said.

"I had two fish. You took them from me and fed five thousand people. I got in trouble for that."

"Yes. I remember you now. Sorry about the fish. I have been eating a lot of fish lately. I don't feel the need to eat at all. But it seems necessary to reassure people that I am here and not a ghost, so I eat. It always seems to be fish. I was with the disciples recently. I cooked breakfast for them. Fish. Lots of fish."

"Could they see you?" she asked.

"They all said they could. But I don't know. Some were looking straight at me, but some were looking just over my shoulder. I think it's my fault."

She asked, "How could that be?"

I wasn't anxious to explain this but I did.

"I have a disciple that everyone calls 'The One I Love.' 'He's the one Joshua loves.' He can absolutely see me. He looks right at me."

"The one that you love?"

"Yes. But it never occurred to me until now what's wrong with that phrase, 'the one that Joshua loves.' The others must know what I think of them."

"What do you mean?"

"Well, different from loved.

"There are disciples I liked.

"There is one I tolerated.

"One who annoyed me.

"One who was not exactly what I would have had him be.

"One whose anger scared me.

"One who always needed me at just the wrong moment.

"One I never told was a second choice.

"How would you like to be known as 'The One Who Was Joshua's Second Choice' or 'The One Joshua Tolerated'?"

"That's normal," the girl said to me. "That's human."

I said, "I don't think so. Not now. It's fear. It's need. I can see what's human now, now that I don't have to fear anything. Now that I don't need anything. Nothing from them, in any case. I can see them as they are. I can't see their faults. I see what they went through to become who they are. And all the things that made me annoyed or discouraged or enraged? I can't even really remember what they were.

"I don't think they can see me clearly because—maybe—I didn't see them clearly.

"I do now.

"I can see how hard they were trying to please me, to compete for my affection. Back then I felt there were only so many hours in the day and I didn't have time for them. Now I have all the time in the world. It hurts me that I didn't see them better.

"Even my mother.

"So much of what I remember about my mother is watching her back as she did her tasks.

"Maybe that's what death taught me.

"To need nothing.

"To fear nothing.

"To sit.

"To look into eyes."

We looked into one another's eyes and she asked, "Why can I see you?"

I said, "Perhaps because we saw one another then. I'm sorry I didn't recognize you at once. How old are you now?"

She said, "fourteen."

I said, "So you would have been eleven at the time. Yes, I can see you now as an eleven-year-old. I remember you now. I remember you looking up at me. Giving me the fish. You ran to bring me the fish. 'Here. Use these.'"

"Your disciples laughed at me. 'Two fish? What can you do with two fish among so many?' You didn't laugh."

"You were giving me everything that you had."

"I got in trouble for that."

"Again, I'm sorry," I said.

"No, it doesn't matter. I would have given you anything. When I saw you I thought I want to grow up to be exactly what you are. In the city people are mean. Or ignore me. You weren't mean. You looked at me like you were glad to see me."

"I was delighted. I still am."

"I thought you might laugh when I gave you the fish."

"Furthest thing from my mind. I remember you. I remember your eyes. I even remember the fish individually."

She said, "So, for a second, we saw one another."

I said, "Perhaps that never goes away. Perhaps that's enough. Perhaps that's all that remains. Perhaps that's the miracle. I mean, five thousand people and not one of them is stopping to greet me. Perhaps we were the miracle."

She said, "I remember you exactly."

I said, "I remember you exactly."

And we stood looking into one another's eyes.

Time passed.

I said, "You must have things to do."

She said, "I don't care."

I said, "You'll get in trouble."

She said, "I don't care. I'll stay as long as you will."

I said, "Careful. I can stay here forever. Literally."

And she said, "That would be fine with me."

And she slipped her hand into mine again.

I said, "You'll have to eat at some point."

She said, "I have some fish. Would you like some fish?"

I said, "Absolutely not."

I asked, "Do you have any bread and wine? That would be refreshing."

And as we ate, standing, facing one another in the street, looking into one another's eyes, "This is my second chance," I thought.

Here.

Where I started.

And five thousand people walked past us.

And I wept for the beauty of the city.

Harrowing Hell

*When they had finished breakfast, Jesus said to Simon
Peter, "Simon son of John, do you love me more than these?
He said to him, "Yes, Lord; you know that I love you."*
                                        —John 21:15

When I asked John if he loved me, he broke down in tears,
saying, "I love you more than life."

When I asked Thomas if he loved me, he said, "I have
trouble with belief, not love. I love you. Never question that."

When I asked Peter if he loved me, he shrugged and
said, "You know."

I said, "Really? 'You know'? That's as far as you're willing
to go?"

He said, "You know."

I said, "You can't bring yourself to just say you love me?"

He said, "You know."

And I thought, "Oh my God. I've put the wrong person
in charge."

Magdalene said, "He's a man. What can you expect?

"Besides, I told you from the start, when you were pick-
them, there were two you couldn't trust, Peter and Judas."

That's true. She had warned me.

I said, "You were only half right. Peter never betrayed me."

She paused for a moment.

Then she said, "No one is telling you this, but he did betray you. The other men ran but Peter followed you. When he was confronted, he said he never knew you."

"Peter said that?"

"Three times."

That explained why Peter had been acting so strangely around me since I returned.

I said, "You called it before it happened."

She said, "This isn't only 'I told you so.' It's also about power. You gave it to him and he's incapable of using it."

I said, "You can't blame me entirely for that. Peter has always thought he is in charge because he owns the boat."

She said, "Well, you'd better do something or the bark of Peter is going to run aground."

I said, "I will."

Then she said, "You're leaving soon, aren't you?"

I said, "Tomorrow."

"Well," she said as she turned her back and walked away, "you'd better get your house in order. Tie up the loose ends."

I knew what I had to do.

I took a skin of wine and went to a hillside and sat by myself until sunset.

I waited until he was sitting next to me.

I offered him the wineskin.

He drank.

I drank.

I said, "It's all right. You can look at me, Judas."

Judas said, "Not yet. It's too painful."

He drank.

He said, "I thought I was ending it all."

I drank.

I said, "I thought for a while they were ending me. But it seems life isn't done with us."

He said, "Have you called me here to punish me?"

I said, "How could I punish you any more than you've punished yourself?"

"Then why am I here?" he asked.

I said, "I need your help."

He said, "With what?"

I said, "You're not the only one who betrayed me."

"Who?"

"Peter," I said.

"Really," he said.

I nodded, "Evidently three times."

"Well," he said, "at least he learns from his mistakes."

We both laughed.

"I need to understand why, and he'll never be able to tell me. He's as inarticulate as you are articulate, so if you can't tell me why you betrayed me, I'll never know. I leave tomorrow and Magdalene says I have to tie up the loose ends."

We were silent. Then Judas said, "I never liked her."

I said, "The feeling was mutual. She's not crazy about Peter either."

I drank.

I asked, "Do you know what they did to me?"

There was silence.

"I'm not asking in order to blame you, to hurt you, to shame you. I just need to know if you are aware of what they did to me."

He nodded and said, "How could you ever love again after someone had done that to you? Not just me. Anyone."

I nodded.

"And yet I do."

He looked at me.

He said, "You know, I never believed I was important to you."

I said, "Well, you're essential now. They can't tell my story without you in it."

He said, "Not the way I'd have chosen to be essential. Still..."

Judas laughed bitterly. Then he drank deeply. Then he drank again.

He said, "I don't seem to be able to get drunk. How am I going to be able to forget?"

He passed me the skin. I drank what little was left.

"There are things I can't forget either. I did not want to come back. The last thing that I saw before dying was a soldier putting a spear in my side. I couldn't defend myself. Why would I return to a world that could do that to me?"

Judas said, "That's how I have felt most of my life."

I said, "I know that now."

After we had sat in silence for a few minutes, I said again, "I did not want to come back. But then the Father spoke to me. In a voice that sounded very much like Joseph's every morning of my boyhood, he said, 'Get up! It's time to get up.' I did not get up. Then he said, in a voice like a thousand Josephs, "Rise. You must rise." I asked, "Why?" And he said, 'I'm not done loving you yet.'"

Then I said, "My friend..."

"Please," Judas said. "Please don't say it."

I said, "I'm not done loving you yet."

And he wept bitterly.

After a while, he asked, "Will I be separated from you forever?"

"Do you wish to be?"

"It might be easier. Facing you is terribly painful."

"For me, too."

"Because I betrayed you?"

"Because I failed you."

He looked at me and said, "I'd like to believe that's the case, but I am afraid this is all mine."

The wine skin was empty, so he stood to go.

As he rose, he asked, "Are the men angry with me?"

"They don't speak of you. You have left a hole behind you. I will work until we are all together again."

"And Magdalene?"

I said, "Don't ask."

He walked a few steps, stopped, turned and looked at me full in the face for the first time, and asked, "What did you say? What exactly did you say to Peter?"

"I asked him if he loved me and if he would feed my sheep."

Judas laughed.

"You were always bad with metaphors, Joshua. No one ever understood your parables. Not even me. The sower and the seeds. The wheat and the weeds."

I said, "Well, I was a carpenter talking to fishermen about agriculture."

Judas grew serious. A teacher. A good one. "Exactly," he said, "Is Peter a shepherd?"

I said, "He's a fisherman."

"And what," he said, "does a fisherman know about sheep? Shepherds care for their sheep. Fishermen don't give a damn about fish. Shepherds will risk their lives for a missing lamb. One fish, more or less, makes no difference to a fisherman. Feed my lambs? What were you thinking? Ask him about fishing."

He started away again.

"I have missed you, Judas."

And he walked into the darkness.

That night, I tried again with Peter with everyone watching.

I said, "Peter, when I'm gone, do you think you can keep this whole crew together in the boat?"

Peter took offense and said, "Are you joking? If any of this lot falls out of the boat, I'm in after them like a shot. I love my crew. I even love you even though you're a bad sailor. We might make a sailor out of you yet."

I asked again, "Will you keep them all in the boat?"

"How can I not?" he said. "I love them."

I asked, "Do you love me, Peter?"

Peter said with passion, "I'd sail into any storm for you. ... Now, are you satisfied?"

I was.

As they walked away, Judas came up beside me.

"How," I asked, "how could you ever believe that I didn't need you?"

After a moment, he said, "Tell me, will you visit me in hell?"

I asked, "Will you visit me in heaven?"

"May I?"

"The door is always open, Judas. You just have to walk through it. The choice is yours, as it always has been. Make a better one this time."

And I walked away to tie up the rest of the loose ends.

Magdalene.

And to say goodbye to my body.

Hard to Leave

Then he led them out as far as Bethany, and, lifting up
his hands, he blessed them. While he was blessing them,
he withdrew from them and was carried up into
heaven.

—Luke 24:50–51

I didn't know it would be this hard to leave.

I have eternity behind me and eternity in front of me. All of it bliss. Angels, seraphim and cherubim. What could thirty-three years have to offer me that I find it so hard leave? Thirty-three years are nothing, though on some hot days, a day could seem very long.

Where did it go?

It seems like yesterday when I first saw all of you.

Peter, you wanted nothing to do with me.

John, you were so young. You've grown so much in three years.

And Magdalene.

The first time I saw her, I was completely dazzled. And she wasn't even trying to dazzle. She was making no effort and she was beyond angels. The first time I saw her I couldn't move. I couldn't speak. And every time after felt like the first time. Before her, I felt ordinary. She made me feel special. As if she saw something special in me. I asked her about this once.

"It wasn't hard," she said, "because it was true." I learned from her how to see people—really see them. Not just glance at them but look into them. So every meeting after that was a moment of stunned presence. What the angels feel toward me, I learned from her to feel toward you.

And you—you are what is making it so hard for me to leave. All of you.

Not just the people I've known all these years. The people I met once. The man born blind and his awful parents. Bartimaeus, son of Timaeus, shouting out, "Son of David, have pity on me" and making a nuisance of himself. Zacchaeus in his absurd tree. The Samaritan woman. So many that are dead now.

How can I love all this that is going to pass so fast and die?

At least angels don't die.

Magdalene explained that's *why* we love and why we love so hard and so deep. Because a human life happens once and goes away. She doesn't understand how it could be possible to love an angel. Why bother? What would be the point? You make no difference to an angel. But a person's life is short and, toward the end, love is like a river forced through a canyon. It becomes intense and fast and churning and wild and that's what I am feeling now at this moment looking at you.

How can I possibly go?

The Samaritan woman and her five husbands. I will miss them. They made a great party together. And, by the way, the Good Samaritan wasn't just a story. He was real. He took care of me when he found me crawling out of the desert starved and dehydrated. Here. See. This is one of the coins he gave me. I have always kept it. And now, as I rise, it won't rise with me. Its weight insists on staying on the earth and it breaks...my...heart.

I am rising.

Against my will, I am being glorified by my Father, and I find myself, not for the first time, shouting at you, but not with anger this time. I am shouting, "*I won't leave you orphans. I will send the spirit.*" But that's not enough.

I shout, "*In my Father's house there are mansions.*"

What a strange thing to shout. I have become a carpenter to my core—huts, sheds, houses, mansions.

"*Mansions. Many mansions. And I will fill them with* you. *How can I enjoy heaven if you aren't there with me? You, who taught me who I am, Peter telling me I am the Messiah. Thomas touching me and making me know I am risen. Magdalene...*"

The problem with remembering the dazzle of the first time is that anything that has a first time has a last time.

Go! Go now! Go to the ends of the earth. Bring them all to me. Find the shepherds. They must be old now. Find the Roman centurion who loved his servant. Bring them to me. Heaven won't be heaven until you are all there with me. Heaven will not be complete without you.

And I find myself making myself foolish, not for the first time, shouting like such an ordinary person...

"*Remember me. Remember me. I will remember you. How could I ever forget you?*"

Acknowledgments

I'm a Jesuit, but I have never successfully made it all the way through the *Spiritual Exercises of Ignatius Loyola.* Not for lack of trying. The wreckage of my retreats is considerable. But Ignatius's Second Week teaches a way of contemplating the life of Christ that has illuminated every day of my life.

Kevin Bradt, SJ, turned Ignatius's method of praying into his style of preaching. Kevin never explained the scriptures. He spoke from within them. I have shamelessly stolen his method. He is in every word of this *Diary,* but his voice, his humor, his beauty are most clear in the chapter titled "Blind Bart."

Kevin could preach the way he did because he had receptive listeners in his community—a descendant of Mike Moynihan's Berkeley Liturgical group. To name a few to stand for all—Kay Lane, Kathleen Tighe, and Andrew Utiger.

You can hear Greg Boyle most clearly in "Give a Child a Scorpion," in which Greg's signature line is put in Jesus's mouth—but that's probably where he got it in the first place, so, fair's fair. In any case, it's hard to tell the difference between the two on a good day. Greg and the Dolores Mission Community, as well as the 17th Street, NYC Jesuit/Mercy/Redemptorist community and our Nativity Schools have shaped my understanding of Jesus.

Mary Galeone, RSM, has shaped my understanding of Magdalene as a something-more-than apostle to the apostles. She was herself and irreplaceable. As is Mary Galeone.

These *Diary* entries were originally homilies written for the early Mass community at Xavier Parish in Manhattan. I thank them for their openness to experimentation, their willingness to laugh and cry at 7:45 in the morning, and their forgiveness when a homily imploded. To name a few to stand for all—Nancy Fava, who first made me aware that these stories might be worth saving by clandestinely recording them; Elda Luisi; and Marjorie Irig. But truly, this *Diary* belongs to them all.

Kevin Bradt's last words to me after fifty years of friendship were, as many of Kevin's sayings were, tragi-comic. He said with a smile and tears, "I don't know how to tell you how much I love you." This could easily be the subtitle of *The Diary* or, for that matter, the Gospels.

And it certainly is how I feel toward those who are the stuff of which this *Diary* is created: Jack Bradt, Kevin's older and wiser brother and my gold standard; Miriam Healey, artist and inspiration; Beth Blickers, agent as creator; a bunch of younger Jesuits who have been kind in reading these as they were written: Rudy Casals, Eric Studt, Ricardo Avila, Luke Hansen, Jack Bentz, Thomas Bambrick, Jake Braithewaite, and others; Nick Weber, mentor and ringmaster of the Royal Lichtenstein Circus; the Boston Shakespeare Company, including Grey Johnson, Cathy Rust, Khorshed Dubash, Steve Aveson, Charlie Marz, Jim Kitendaugh, Marjorie Tucker, Norman Frisch, Peter McLoughlin; David and Arla Manson; Robert Egan and the Ojai Playwrights Conference, my artistic home; the casts and crews of all the plays; all my Jesuit communities.

And Orbis—especially Paul McMahon and Celine Allen.